Soft Furnishing Workshops

Cushions
and Pillows

Soft Furnishing Workshops

Cushions
and Pillows

Professional
skills made easy

hamlyn

Contents

First published in Great Britain
in 2001 by
Hamlyn, an imprint of Octopus
Publishing Group Ltd
2-4 Heron Quays, London E14 4JP

Distributed in the United States and
Canada by
Sterling Publishing Co., Inc.
387 Park Avenue South,
New York, NY 10016-8810

ISBN 0 600 60231 1

A CIP catalogue record for this book
is available from the British Library

Printed and bound in China

This book first appeared as part of
The Hamlyn Book of Soft Furnishings

Metric and imperial measurements
Both metric and imperial measurements have
been given in the instructions throughout this
book. You should choose to work in either metric
or imperial, but do not mix the measurements
to ensure your projects' success.

Introduction

WHILE SOFT FURNISHINGS such as curtains and rugs help to create a room's style, cushions are an important accessory. If you make your own, your use of different fabrics, textures, patterns, details and colour combinations ensure that no one else will ever have your furnishing style. A single cushion can be carefully planned to give just the right balance of size, shape, colour and texture to create a certain impact on its own, or two or more cushions might be designed to work together on a plain background.

Setting the style

The details that make up a room's style include everything from the wall and floor finishes to ornaments and flower arrangements, all of which work together for a cohesive and pleasing interior design scheme. Fabrics and soft furnishings need to be chosen to suit the overall design scheme, and can make a major style statement in any room. Experiment with colour and furnishing schemes until you find the one that suits you. By learning how to mix and match colours, patterns, textures

and accessories, and by following your own design instincts, you will soon create a happy and attractive mix in your home.

If you want a starting point for a style to suit your home, you might think about the particular interests and passions in your life, so that you can build up a style around a theme. If you love gardening, a floral theme or leafy green colours can set the style of a room. If you enjoy travel, you can have fun planning your room schemes around different countries – think about developing a richly coloured Indian living room or a sunny French kitchen. Alternatively, build a room scheme around a favourite collection of antiques or ornaments, choosing paints, wallpapers and fabrics to blend in with the collection's colours. The options are limited only by your imagination.

Cushion styles

Cushions and pillows come in a huge range of styles. Probably the most common types are scatter cushions – small accessories that can really make a big impact. Imagine a neutral living room furnished with textures and tones of creams and stone and the impression that just a single lime

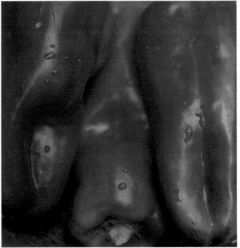

Left *Cushions and pillows are perfect soft furnishing accessories. They can be mixed and matched – for size, shape, colour and fabric – to add decorative style and comfort to beds, chairs and sofas.*

Top right *Foreign travel can provide you with inspiration for the colours or theme of an interior decorating scheme.*

Centre and bottom right *The colours and textures of nature have a large part to play in the decorating palette and can offer a starting point for a particular style to suit your home.*

green satin cushion on one chair will make; or think about the same room with a row of stunning hyacinth-blue silk cushions standing up along the back of the sofa. A basic scatter cushion can become a focal point on furniture and does not necessarily need any adornment. However, if you don't want to leave your cushions plain, you can embellish them with fringes, tassels, cords and buttons, or with fancy closures.

Decorative, practical and versatile, scatter cushions can be used in many different rooms in your home with different effect. Give a single cushion prominence in an elegant chair in a study or on a wicker chair in a large bathroom, mass them on a squashy sofa, place them in colourful piles in children's playrooms or arrange them decoratively on a bed.

Above *The seams of a plain sofa are piped with a green striped fabric to match that used for some of the cushions and for the low footstool that doubles as a coffee table. The striped cushions coordinate cleverly with the teaset design.*

Designs in pillows are endless, too. Large round bolsters, huge square pillows, frilled, bordered, tasselled and fringed pillows and embroidered or heart-shaped pillows all work well, piled on a bed. Comfortable 'bedheads' can be made with slim boxed cushions, fitted to a pole behind the bed or hung by ribbons tied to small decorative coat hooks. Alternatively, make two quilted and stuffed large bordered pillows to prop up against a less comfortable wooden or cane headboard.

Seating styles

Cushions other than large floor cushions and bean bags can be piled on the floor for when additional seating is required. For use outdoors, make large scatter cushions or stripy boxed cushions in mixed, washable fabrics to place on a sun terrace or decking. For a touch of elegance indoors, make three or four boxed cushions in richly coloured damasks, add decorative cord and tasselled corners and pile them in a corner of an elegant living room.

Seat cushions are mostly made with a firm inner pad, to soften a hard surface and to give support. Buttoning and piping along the seams in a contrasting tone against the main fabric give seat cushions a strong identity and a stylish look. This more tailored look works especially well with metal and wooden chairs, and looks effective on window seats, too.

Less formal chair styles, such as wicker chairs and soft sofas need softer cushions. More feminine fabrics and lighter colours, frills and self-covered toning piping can look good here. Detailed ties and ruching can also be appropriate with less formal treatments.

Colour schemes

Neutral and all white rooms may be 'traditional' or 'contemporary' in style and the colours and design of the accessories can emphasize or detract from the period or the modern look. A single cushion in shocking pink can make a huge impact on an all-white room; a cushion with a small white and pale lilac print makes little impact, but can help lead the way for other patterns and colours.

Above *A love of antique fabrics and early prints is the style source for this bedroom. Toile de Jouy and hand-embroidered pillows sit against simple block checks, all of which blend with the antique hand-quilted bedcover.*

Left *This informal-style, rounded wicker chair needs a soft, comfortable cushion rather than a firm seat cushion. Since the cushion is used alone, it can afford to be quite striking.*

Monochromatic room schemes can be very restful to live with. Use different textures for cushions (such as matt linen, shot silk, crunchy-textured woven wool, fine cottons and self-patterned jacquards), and employ lighter and darker tones to offer variety.

Durable fabrics

For cushion-making, always choose fabric that will wear and clean well. If possible, buy fabrics made from natural fibres and always wash all washable cover fabrics before making up. Seat cushions in particular should be machine washable. Consider using fabrics not normally used for cushion-making – unbleached linen, denim, artists' canvas, fine woven jute, gingham, woven rugs and kelims, old knitted pullovers or mattress ticking for example.

Above *Pattern on pattern always creates a style of its own. Here, soft pinks and whites combine to include naive embroidery motifs, hand-woven lace and toile de Jouy prints of country scenes.*

Decorative finishes

Cords, braids, tassels and fringes all add style and elegance to any cushion or pillow. Look out for special antique or antique-style trimmings with beads and toggles, too. Simple ricrac braid or soft patterned Tyrolean woven braids can blend well with country fabrics.

Stencilled designs and appliqué motifs can also liven up a plain fabric. Pick up a motif from a fabric or wallpaper border, or use a classical stencil such as an everlasting Greek key motif, and centre it in your cushion cover.

Ideas and projects

CUSHIONS AND PILLOWS are often used as accessories, grouped together on a plain sofa or a bed to make a striking focal point. They are simple to make, can be easily moved around and are fairly inexpensive so the covers can be changed frequently.

Try making cushion covers in versatile cottons and linens or in more sumptuous velvets or damasks; customize them by adding trimmings, piping, buttons or beads to complement the room's decorative style. You can also make large floor cushions, bolsters or even boxed cushions to revive an old sofa. Make pillowcases to suit your bedroom style – coloured borders to tone in with a duvet cover, frills or lace to provide a soft, romantic appeal.

Shapes and fillings

EVERY CUSHION NEEDS a good cushion pad. You can either buy ready-made cushion pads or make your own. There are many fillings and fabrics available for making your own pads and you can make them to fit unusual seats or cushion covers.

Ready-made cushion pads come in many shapes and sizes. Firm seat cushions are normally made from fire-retardant foam, which can be covered with cotton or polyester wadding to soften the lines. If you like a firm seat but prefer a softer look, try making a mini feather quilt to wrap around the foam. For soft scatter cushions, choose between feather/down and firmer polyester fillings. Traditional kapok (cotton wadding) is less practical, but helps to give a firmly stuffed cushion.

If you cannot find a ready-made scatter cushion pad of a suitable shape or size for your needs, buy heavy-duty featherproof cambric to make your own (see below). Buy loose feathers and down, or use polyester fibre filling.

Above *Cushions need to be slightly under-filled for comfort. Feather and down cushions mould readily to shape and also plump up again easily.*

Right *The cover for a display cushion can be chosen for its beauty rather than practicality. Cushions used for display or decoration are usually over-filled and plump.*

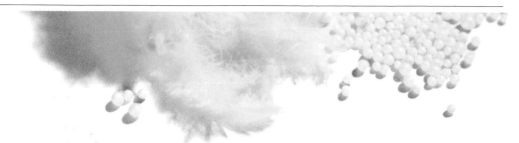

Feather-filled cushion pad

MEASUREMENTS

Size of finished cushion pad:
50cm (20in) square

SUGGESTED FABRICS

Featherproof cambric or ticking

MATERIALS

Fabric for cover – 0.7m (¾yd)
of 120cm (48in) wide fabric

Loose feathers or feather/down
filling

Scissors and sewing equipment

Matching sewing thread

Above and below *Loose
feathers and down, kapok and
polystyrene beads are just some
of the various cushion fillings
that are available.*

If you need a cushion pad for a
special seat or a cushion cover
that is an irregular shape or an
unusual size, make your own
cushion pad to fit as follows.

MAKING THE PAD COVER

Cut two panels of fabric, 50cm
(20in) square. Place the right
sides together with the raw
edges matching. Taking a 12mm
(½in) seam, stitch around three
sides of the cover, and continue
the seam for 5cm (2in) at each
end of the longer open edge.
Repeat to make a double line
of stitching to prevent the
feather filling coming out at
the seams. Clip the corners, turn
the cover the right side out and
press, turning under the seam
allowance along the open edge
and pressing.

FILLING AND FINISHING

Carefully fill the pad with
feathers, pushing them well
into the corners. Use plenty of
filling for a plump cushion. Pin
the folded seam allowances
together. Slipstitch or topstitch
the opening to secure the filling
in place firmly. It is now ready
for inserting in a cushion cover.

Gussetted cushion cover

MATERIALS

Block of fire-retardant foam, about 5cm (2in) thick, cut to seat size

Cotton lining fabric to cover foam (see cutting instructions)

Medium-weight polyester wadding (see cutting instructions)

Scissors and sewing equipment

Matching sewing thread

Below *Permanent covers fitted to foam blocks. Piping along the seams emphasizes the shape of the covers.*

To cover a foam block, for a chair or window seat for example, make a permanent covering of lining or calico before making the top cover. A layer of wadding softens the shape.

MEASURING UP AND CUTTING OUT

Measure each face of the foam block. Cut a panel of lining fabric for each face, adding a 2.5cm (1in) seam allowance around each panel. Cut a piece of wadding: the measurement in one direction should be twice the foam's width, plus the depth, plus 2.5cm (1in) for overlap; the measurement in the other direction should be the foam's length, plus the depth, plus 5cm (2in) for two overlaps.

WRAPPING THE FOAM

Wrap the wadding around the foam, positioning the overlap at one side. Use large basting stitches to hold the wadding in place. Fold over the ends, tucking in excess wadding at the corners, and stitch down the edge of the wadding to hold it in place at front and back.

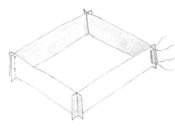

FITTING THE TOP AND BOTTOM PANELS

Reposition the gusset around the foam block, wrong side out, and lay the top panel over the foam block. Pin this panel to the gusset all around the edges. Turn the foam over and repeat for the back panel, leaving one edge open so that you can remove the cover. Stitch all the pinned seams. Trim the seam allowances and trim all excess fabric from the corners. Press the fabric, turning under and pressing the seam allowances along the open edge. Turn the cover the right side out and push out the corners neatly using the tip of a pair of scissors. Insert the

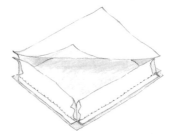

foam through the opening (unpick the gusset seams at the opening if the foam is too thick or firm). Stitch up the opening by hand, or topstitch it by machine if you can slip the folded seam allowances under the foot of the machine.

MAKING THE GUSSET

Position the four lining gusset pieces, wrong side out, along the side faces of the foam block. Pin the seams at the corners. Remove from the foam and stitch the corner seams. The seam length should match the foam depth only and not extend into the seam allowance. Trim the seam allowances. Press the seams open.

Choosing cushion pads and fillings

- Curled poultry feathers or duck feathers are the least expensive feather filling.

- A mix of either 85/15 or 51/49 feather and down gives a softer, more comfortable cushion, especially for chair back cushions and pillows.

- Acrylic fibre fillings do not give a lasting shape, but are useful for people who are allergic to feathers.

- Sofa seat and back cushions need high-quality fillings and should be channelled with several pockets to keep the filling evenly distributed.

- Feathers do not last forever – they will uncurl and flatten so that they will not plump up at all. Replace the pad rather than trying to revive them.

- Use featherproof cambric or ticking to make up your own cushion pads with feather/down fillings. Cushion pads with cotton, polyester and foam fillings can be made up in lining material or sheeting.

- Make sure any foam that you use is fire retardant.

- Wrap foam cushions in wadding and make a cover of curtain lining or calico to prevent the cushion fabric rubbing.

- Polystyrene beads are a firm filling for floor cushions. Once enclosed in a cover, the beads hold their shape well.

Closures and fastenings

ALTHOUGH ZIPS are convenient, there are other options for closing a cushion cover; the fastening you choose depends on whether you want to make a feature of it, or keep it as unobtrusive as possible. Buttons and ties can add a decorative touch, while ready-made tapes (with press studs or hooks and eyes) are a discreet alternative to a zip. The simplest cushion covers have no closure at all – the opening is simply slipstitched closed after inserting the pad.

The cushion cover opening should be the same width as the cushion, to make it easy to insert the pad. With rectangular cushions, it is more economical to make the opening across the width rather than down the length, since less of the specific fastening will be required. It also makes the opening less obtrusive. The seam allowance and/or overlap between the back panels along the opening depends on the type of closure (see box opposite).

Zips, tapes and buttons

Zips and ready-made tapes are the most usual choice of closure. These can be inserted along a seam line, but it is much simpler to set them into a panel of fabric for the back of the cover.

Buttons are enjoying a revival as both decoration and closure. Old-fashioned pillowslips were often just rectangular bags, with buttons and buttonholes along matching hemmed edges at the opening. For a more decorative buttoned opening, the cushion cover or pillowcase can be stitched on three sides, with a lined flap along the opening edge. Work bound or machine-stitched buttonholes in the flap, or stitch button loops along the edge. The flap may be pointed or rectangular , or be held with a set of buttons or a single button.

Other fastenings

Ties are easy to make and more decorative than zips. Make long thin lengths for trailing floppy bows, short wide ties for proud bows, or fine 'tubes' of fabric known as rouleaux (see pages 67 and 68). Instead of fabric ties, ready-made ribbons, binding tapes, cotton webbing and decorative braids could all be substituted; these would need

Above *This envelope-style cushion cover has no fastening at all – just a large tuck-in flap that holds the cushion pad in place.*

Left *Discreet zip fastenings do not detract from the appearance of cushion covers and allow the covers to be removed easily when they need cleaning.*

READY-MADE CLOSURES

Type of closure	Details	When to use	Seam/turning allowances
Zips	Available in a wide range of colours and lengths, and three or four different weights in plastic or metal.	Forms an unobtrusive closure on any type of cushion. Use chunky metal zips on large floor cushions, lightweight dressmaking zips around the seam of a circular cushion.	Allow a 2cm (¾in) seam allowance down either side of the opening where the zip is to be inserted.
Hook-and-eye tape	Available by the metre or yard in two or three widths and weights. The eyes may be in the form of metal bars or a series of eyelets down the length of the tape.	Particularly suitable for tailored covers – on foam seat cushions or boxed sofa cushions, for example.	On the underlapping edge, allow the width of the tape plus a turning half the width of the tape. On the overlapping edge, allow a turning half the width of the tape. Topstitch the tape in place on the right side of the underlap and the wrong side of the overlap, enclosing turnings.
Press-stud tape	As for hook-and-eye tape. Studs may be plastic or metal.	Use on tailored covers. Use lightweight tapes with plastic studs on bed pillows.	As for hook-and-eye tape.

only cutting and hemming to contain any fraying.

Since completely washable upholstery fabrics are limited, and any plain colour will show stains, making covers to tie over seat cushions is a stylish way of keeping them clean – especially in family rooms. Over covers – just rectangles of washable fabric such as cotton piqué, with ties stitched to two sides – may be laundered and easily replaced. You could also quilt the over covers, backing the top fabric with ticking to make them reversible.

Right *A cushion cover fastened with one or more buttons along its flap should not be overfilled so it bulges around the opening, as this can look unsightly.*

Scatter cushion with zip

MEASUREMENTS

Size of cushion pad:
40cm (16in) square

Size of finished cushion cover:
38cm (15in) square

SUGGESTED FABRICS

Glazed cotton is used here, but almost any fabric is suitable

MATERIALS

40cm (16in) square cushion pad

Fabric for cover – 0.5m (½yd) of 120cm (48in) wide fabric

33cm (13in) zip

Scissors and sewing equipment

Matching sewing thread

MEASURING UP AND CUTTING OUT

Measure the cushion pad from seam to seam. The cover should be 2cm (1in) smaller in each direction for a snug fit. Allow a 1.5cm (⅝in) seam allowance on three sides and 2.5cm (1in) on the opening edge. Cut out two pieces of fabric, placing any pattern to its best advantage.

INSERTING THE ZIP

Press 2.5cm (1in) to the wrong side of fabric along what will be

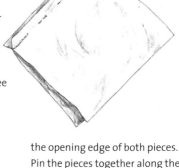

the opening edge of both pieces. Pin the pieces together along the pressed line and stitch for just 4cm (1½in) at each end. Insert the zip (see page 66).

Right *A single scatter cushion in a fresh, summery, floral print brings light relief between two plain blue cushions.*

> ## Tip
> Caring for soft furnishings as part of your cleaning routine prolongs their life and improves the look of a room. Plump up pillows and cushions daily, particularly if they are filled with feather and down, so that they keep their shape and look good for longer.

Making a quartered cushion cover

Cut some spare fabric to finished cushion size to use as a template. Fold along the diagonals and cut to make four small triangles, or fold and cut so as to make four squares or rectangles. Place these on your chosen fabrics, keeping the grain straight and cut out the shapes, adding a 1.5cm (⅝in) seam allowance all around.

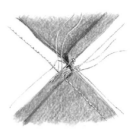

Join the pieces in pairs by machine stitching along the seam allowance. Press the seams open. With right sides facing, match the two stitched pieces of fabric at what will be the centre of the cushion, pushing a pin through both joins to hold securely.

Pin from the centre towards each outer edge, then machine stitch from the centre to each edge in turn. As you return to the centre for the second seam insert the needle exactly where the last stitch finished. Do not backstitch, but leave long threads in the centre. Pull the threads through, knot and stitch through one seam to secure. Press the seam flat and continue to make up as a basic cushion cover (see opposite).

JOINING THE PANELS

Pin the remaining three sides together, right sides facing, taking care to match the corners. Open up the zip halfway and stitch around the remaining three sides, 1.5cm (⅝in) in from the raw edges. Snip across each corner to within 6mm (¼in) of the stitching line. Neaten the raw edges and turn the cover the right side out. Push out the corners neatly using the tip of a pair of scissors if necessary. Press each seam carefully from the front and insert the cushion pad.

Right *Basic scatter cushions need no fancy decorative extras. The simplest ones have zip fastenings, provide comfort for easy lounging and can be useful in the room's colour scheme.*

Envelope-style cushion

SUGGESTED FABRICS

Cotton is used here, but almost any fabric is suitable

MATERIALS

Fabric for cover and ties (see cutting instructions)

Cushion pad

Scissors and sewing equipment

Matching sewing thread

This attractive simple slip-over style of cover has just one opening edge, secured with ties, with a tuck-in flap, made in a similar way to a pillowcase.

MEASURING UP AND CUTTING OUT

Cut out front and back pieces from the fabric to match the cushion pad, allowing an extra 1.5cm (⅝in) for seam allowances. Cut two pieces of fabric to act as facings, 12.5cm (5in) wide and 3cm (1¼in) longer than the opening side. Place any pattern to its best advantage. Cut two or three pairs of ties, 25 × 5cm (10 × 2in) for knotted ties or 46 × 2cm (18 × ¾in) for floppy bows. Use more ties for larger cushions.

FITTING TIES AND FACINGS

Make up the ties (see page 68). Position them on the right side of the front panel of fabric, along what will be the cushion cover's opening edge. The raw ends of the ties should match the raw edge of the front panel. Pin in place. Place one of the facings on top, right sides together, sandwiching the ends of the ties between the two pieces of fabric. Pin then stitch along the seam line. Double stitch over each tie to provide extra strength. Repeat for the back panel.

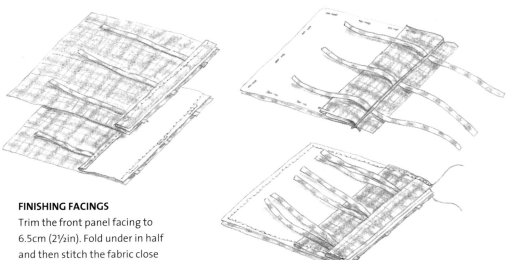

FINISHING FACINGS

Trim the front panel facing to 6.5cm (2½in). Fold under in half and then stitch the fabric close to the fold. To neaten the raw back edge of the back facing, turn under 12mm (½in) to the wrong side and then stitch in place. Turn the facings to the wrong side of the panels and then press them in place.

JOINING THE FRONT AND BACK PANELS

With the right sides facing, pin the back panel to the front panel, but open out the front panel facing, then fold and pin it over the back panel. Stitch the side and end seams. Clip all the corners, and then turn the cover the right side out. Push out the corners using the tip of a pair of scissors then press each seam well and insert the cushion pad.

Above left *In a pile of assorted blue and white cushions, the casual ties of one provide a striking point of interest.*

Right *These simply knotted, short ties and the inner flap are made in a contrasting colour to the main fabric.*

Rouleau loop-and-button closure

SUGGESTED FABRICS

Cotton is used here, but almost any fabric is suitable

MATERIALS

Fabric for cover (see cutting instructions)

Cushion pad

Soft pencil

A length of rouleau (see page 67), three times the length of the cushion

Fabric-covered or rounded buttons, one per 2cm (¾in) or one per 6cm (2¼in)

Iron-on or sew-in interfacing (optional)

Scissors and sewing equipment

Matching sewing thread

MEASURING UP AND CUTTING OUT

Cut a fabric panel for the cushion front, 3cm (1¼in) larger than the cushion pad; a panel for the cushion back, 3cm (1¼in) larger than the pad plus 7.5cm (3in) wider along the opening side, and a 7.5cm (3in) wide strip to form a facing the length of the cushion.

FITTING THE ROULEAU LOOPS

On the fabric panel that will be the cushion front, mark 2cm (¾in) gaps with soft pencil, along the opening side. Divide the rouleau length into sections of 6.5cm (2½in), or more for

larger buttons. Pin each section to the cushion front between the pencil marks, lining up all the raw edges. Stitch along the seam line to hold the rouleau loops in place.

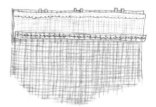

POSITIONING FACING

Pin the fabric facing strip over the rouleau loops, matching the seam allowances and stitch just inside the last stitching line, so that no stitching shows from the front and the rouleau loops are sandwiched in place. Fold the facing's raw edge under to the wrong side by 6mm (¼in) and stitch to neaten.

Applying interfacing

Press fabric to be interfaced before applying interfacing to the fabric's wrong side. When applying fusible (iron-on) interfacing, protect the sole plate of the iron and ensure the iron does not over-heat the interfacing by using a pressing cloth between the iron and interfacing. For sew-in

interfacing, baste it to the main fabric and use the two as though a single layer. Trim all the interfacing from the seam allowances, close to the seam line.

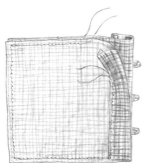

JOINING THE FRONT AND BACK

Pin the front and back pieces together, right sides facing. Neaten the raw edges of the opening edge of the back panel by pressing 6mm (¼in) to the wrong side and stitching close to the fold line. Fold this piece over

again and pin securely. Stitch three sides along the seam allowance. Trim across each corner, neaten the seams and turn the cover the right side out. Push out the corners using the tip of a pair of scissors and press.

ADDING CLOSURES

Mark the button positions with pins and stitch the buttons in place. If the fabric is fine or might tear easily, insert an interfacing along the length of the opening (see box opposite) or stitch each button into a reinforcing neatened square of fabric. Insert the cushion pad and button up.

Above *Rouleau loop-and-button closures are a sophisticated feature on cushion covers. You can make fabric rouleaux or purchase ribbon or tapes for ease.*

Trimmings

BUTTONS AND BOWS, ribbons and braids, cords and piping, frills and fringes, rosettes and tassels can all add a distinctive touch to your cushions. Buy ready-made trimmings or make them up yourself to coordinate with other soft furnishings. Use them to add bold accents of colour or ornamentation, to add a feminine touch or a soft country look.

When planning soft furnishings, think about selecting fabrics and building up colour schemes. If you cannot find ready-made piping and braids to match your fabric, make up your own binding or frills and ties.

Build up a colour board of fabric swatches and samples – you can even try out the effects with offcuts of fabric, making up your own details to trim your covers.

Trimmings fall into two main categories: they may be topstitched to the front panel of a cushion cover or inserted in the seams around the edge. Trimmings that need to be topstitched include woven braids, lace, ribbons and fine cords – you can even cut fabric strips to stitch across the front of a cover. For example, a chunky wool fan-edged braid stitched to woven horsehair immediately makes what is a rather stiff fabric appear softer and more interesting; while ricrac braid gives a cheerful touch to a cushion in a child's bedroom. Topstitched trimmings are usually added to the cushion's front panel before the cover is made up (see pages 72–73), or they may be used to accentuate a topstitched seam line on a flat-bordered cover.

Top *An eclectic mix of plaids and checks in blues, greens and mauves, featuring chenille ruched fringing and piping.*

Above *A multicoloured fringe is very much in keeping with the bright, patterned style of this tapestry cushion.*

Around a cushion's seam lines, you can add crisp piping, gathered frills, lace or broderie anglaise. Mix and match trimmings, emphasizing a frilled pillow with piping or, for a softer touch, combine a narrow, gathered lace trimming with a frill of crisp, floral chintz.

Ready-made trimmings

Bought trimmings are available in many styles and colours. Specialist companies will even make some to order – from simple walling braid to elaborate period tasselled fringes. You can also find fantastic antique braids and fringes in bric-à-brac shops.

Buttons can form the closure for cushion covers (see pages 20–23), but can also be used as trimmings. Cover special button forms (see page 68) in fabric to match the piping on a boxed cushion, for example, or add buttons in wood or bone and tassels to trim a flat-bordered cushion. Rosettes, too, can add extra detail (see page 27).

Above left *Pink fan-edged trimming offsets the colours in this bold plaid cushion.*

Left *Cushions in plain neutral coloured fabrics are good foils for colourful trimmings, as here.*

Making a tassel

MEASUREMENTS

Size of tassel: 5cm (2in) long

SUGGESTED YARN

Any yarn, from knitting wool
to stranded embroidery cotton

MATERIALS

Piece of stiff card, 10cm (4in)
square

Yarn

Bodkin

Scissors

MAKING UP THE TASSEL

Fold the card in half. Wind yarn
around the card until you have
the desired thickness
for your tassel. Cut
several strands of yarn
about 20cm (8in) long.
Twist them
together, then
use a bodkin to
thread them
under the
strands of tassel
on one side of the card.

yarn off the card and cut the
strands of tassel furthest
from the knot.

MAKING THE TASSEL LOOP

Tie the ends together, then pull
the knot under the
threads of tassel. Tie
a knot in the loops
of thread,
tightening it
against the
tassel. Slide the

BINDING THE TASSEL

Take another length of yarn and
use it to bind the
head of the tassel
tightly by wrapping
it half a dozen times
around the tassel near the
top. Knot the free ends of the
yarn together firmly and trim.

Above *There is huge scope for
mixing and matching cushion
shapes, sizes, colours and fabrics,
as well as trimmings – chenille
tassels, topstitched braid and
silky rope-twist insertion cord
have been used here.*

Above *A professionally made tassel adds a distinctive finish to a ruched bolster.*

Left *Tassels, woven braid and chenille cord add interest to these Medieval-style cushions.*

Making a rosette

MEASUREMENTS

Size of rosette (finished diameter): 10cm (4in)

SUGGESTED FABRICS

Corded silk, glazed cotton or folded ribbon. This trimming is not suited to heavy fabrics

MATERIALS

Strip of fabric 40 × 12.5cm (16 × 5in), i.e. four times the finished diameter by twice the radius, plus a 12mm (½in) seam allowance

Fabric-covered button (optional – see page 68)

Scissors and sewing equipment

Matching sewing thread

MAKING UP THE ROSETTE

Fold your chosen fabric in half lengthways, right sides together. Stitch a 12mm (½in) seam along the open edge, Trim, then press the seam flat, centring the seam along the length of the band. Turn the band the right side out. Press. Fold and press a 12mm (½in) turning at one open raw edge and then slipstitch to the opposite end to make a ring.

GATHERING THE ROSETTE

Stitch a line of gathering stitches along one folded edge of the rosette, 6mm (¼in) in from the fold line. Then gather up the thread tightly, flattening out the fabric to form a rosette. Secure the gathering threads with some backstitches. Finish the rosette with a fabric-covered button in the centre, if required.

Piping and frills

PIPING THE OUTER EDGE of a cushion can make it much more stylish and interesting. Striped fabrics cut on the cross give a striking finish, as do checked fabrics cut on the diagonal. On a single cushion the exact colour and size of a piped, defined edge can be crucial; for example, the piping on cushions in an informal pile should be subtle and not too distinctive.

Frilled edges give cushions a softer, feminine look and work particularly well in floral fabric and with bedroom furnishings. Made in the same fabric as the cushion cover, frill can be piped and bound with a contrasting colour, a striped edge can be combined with a floral print, or double frills can go with large and small prints or checks and stripes.

Piped cushion

SUGGESTED FABRICS

Glazed cotton, colour-woven stripes and checks, and many other fabrics are suitable. The piped edges of cushions and covers wear quickly so check that the quality of fabric used for the piping is at least as good as the main fabric

MATERIALS

Fabric for cover (see cutting instructions)

Cushion pad

Fabric and cord for piping (see page 69) to go all around cover, plus overlap

Zip to match cushion pad width

Scissors and sewing equipment

Matching sewing thread

Plain piping on a patterned cover gives it distinction and helps to define its shape and size.

MEASURING UP AND CUTTING OUT

Cut two pieces of main fabric 3cm (1¼in) wider and 5cm (2in) longer than the required cover,

placing any pattern centrally in the panels. Make up enough piping to go around the cushion circumference (see page 69).

POSITIONING THE PIPING

Press 3.5cm (1⅜in) to the wrong side on both lower edges of the cushion cover. Pin the piping to

Right *Selecting a single colour for the piping on a patterned cushion can be difficult – pick a favourite or one to coordinate with another colour in the room.*

the cushion front, starting at the centre bottom, lining up the piping stitching line with the fold line along the opening and aligning the raw edges on the other three sides. Clip into the piping fabric at the corners to keep them square and overlap the fabric at the join neatly (see page 70).

INSERTING THE ZIP

Stitching as close to the piping as possible, join the front to the back along the lower edge, for just 4cm (1½in) at each end. Insert the zip (see page 66).

MAKING UP THE COVER

Join the other three sides. Stitch as close to the piping as possible.

Turn to the front to check that none of the piping stitching still shows. If it does, restitch again even closer. Clip the corners and neaten the raw edges. Turn the cushion cover the right side out and push out the corners using the tip of a pair of scissors. Press, then insert the cushion pad.

Above *Piping in the same fabric as the cushion cover provides a smart tailored look ideal for more formal settings.*

Left *A pale cushion with a bold motif uses a contrast for the piping – a smart black and white striped fabric similar to that used on the armchair.*

Frill-edged cushion

SUGGESTED FABRICS

Cotton, glazed cotton or sateen, colour-woven stripes and checks

MEASUREMENTS

Size of finished frill: 6cm (2¼in) for a 40cm (16in) cushion; 7.5cm (3in) for a 46cm (18in) cushion; 9cm (3½in) for a 50cm (20in) cushion

MATERIALS

Fabric for cover and for frill (see cutting instructions)

Cushion pad

Fabric and cord for piping (see page 69) to go all around cover, plus overlap

Zip to match cushion pad width

Scissors and sewing equipment

Matching sewing thread

If you have made a cushion that looks a little small, adding a frill will give it more prominence. Frilled edges may be short and crisp or long and floppy, but should always be at least double fullness.

CUTTING OUT AND PREPARING THE FRILL

Cut out the cushion cover front, the back and the piping from the main fabric, as for the Piped Cushion (see page 28). For the frill, cut out and join together fabric strips to make one long strip that measures twice the circumference of the cushion by twice the finished width, allowing 4cm (1½in) for seam allowances on the frill.

MAKING THE FRILL

Stitch the two short ends together to make a continuous loop at least twice the cushion circumference; press all the seams flat. Fold the frill strip in half lengthways, right side out. Stitch two rows of gathering stitches 1.5cm (⅝in) and 2cm (¾in) from the raw edge.

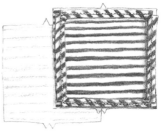

POSITIONING THE PIPING

Cut and notch the front and back pieces of the cover so as to mark the edges to be joined. Make up enough piping to go around the cushion circumference (see page 69). Stitch the piping to the front piece of the cushion cover, as for the Piped Cushion.

Above *These very long frills are overtly feminine.*

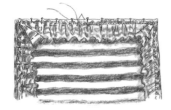

GATHERING THE FRILL

Fold the frill into four and mark the quarters with pins. Pull the gathering threads and distribute the frill evenly around the cushion cover front, aligning the pins with the corners and pinning the frill along the seam line, the pins at right angles to the raw edges. Stitch along the seam line, as close to the piping as possible. Check from the front and stitch again, closer in, if necessary. Stitch the back of the cover to the front, insert the zip, and finish as for the Piped Cushion.

Above *A frill softens the look of a cushion but used, as here, in a simple gingham, it need not necessarily look fussy.*

More options for making frills

SINGLE FRILL Use a fabric strip the desired finished width of the frill, plus 2.7cm (1⅛in) for turnings and seams, its length twice the circumference of the cushion. Make a 6mm (¼in) double hem along one long edge and stitch gathering threads along the other.

DOUBLE FRILL Make two frills as above, the outer frill 1.5cm (⅝in) wider than the inner. Pin the raw edges together, stitch gathering threads through both frills to make up as one.

BOUND FRILLS Cut two strips of main fabric for the frill, each the desired finished frill width plus 2cm (¾in). Cut a strip of contrasting fabric the same length and 4.5cm (1¾in) wide. Stitch a frill length to each long side of this strip, right sides together, 1cm (⅜in) in from the raw edges. Press the seams to the centre then press the frill in half along the centre line, so that the binding shows equally each side. Stitch gathering threads as before.

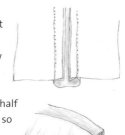

Buttons and beads

ELABORATE BEADING and decorative buttoning are used extensively in the world of *haute couture* to enhance clothing. With thoughtful imagination and research, a few carefully placed decorative beads or buttons can really turn a simple cushion into something special, too. Look through photographs of couture collections, magazine features and advertising brochures, and make a file of tear sheets and notes to bring colours, textures and shapes together ready for adaptation to cushion fronts. Historical pattern and ornament reference books as well as transfer books from craft and art shops will help with finding classical shapes.

Buttons have long been the secret weapon of the fashion world, and searching out a medium-priced, well-cut jacket and simply changing the buttons to raise the profile is a well-known trick. When it comes to using buttons as fastenings for cushions (see pages 34–35), there are many possibilities. Paper-like taffeta and crunchy silks buttoned with mother of pearl, cashmere with gold drops or silk brocade with ribbon balls all express sheer luxury. Try teaming white cotton with blue glass, navy blue wool with plaid buttons, plaids with blazer buttons and suiting tweed with leather knots for decorative scatter cushions. You could even fasten traditional highland tartan with kilt pins.

Beaded cushions

Plain or embroidered cushions can be livened up with a beaded design. Select a design you like, then translate it into something workable. Magazines, books and photographs are all good sources for inspiration. An abstract design might catch your eye, a pastoral scene or a specific geometric pattern. Embroidery books will also be useful to help you put your ideas on to paper.

Choose your cushion cover fabric and cut out the front and back panels. Draw your design freehand on a fabric panel, using a soft drawing pencil or tailor's chalk. Mark out the design's pattern using glass-headed dressmaker's pins to represent each bead. Stitch one bead at a time, removing each pin in turn. Secure each bead in place with a backstitch using sewing thread the same colour as the bead.

When the bead design is finished, make up the cushion cover according to your choice of style (see pages 16–21) and insert a cushion pad to finish.

Right *Embroidered silks or textured fabrics go beautifully with tiny beads to make an unusual decorative cushion.*

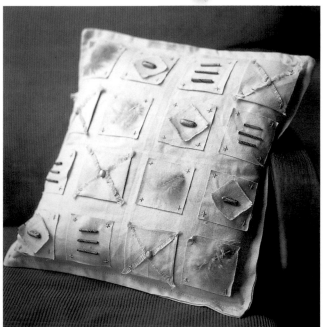

Above *Many different types of beads can be used to decorate cushions. Buy unusual styles when you see them and keep them in a bead box to be pulled out when you need them.*

Left *Small sea shells, feathers and assorted odds and ends offer scope for unusual and novel decoration for cushion fronts.*

Buttoned lined cushion

SUGGESTED FABRICS

A cotton/linen mix is used here, but almost any fabric is suitable

MATERIALS

Fabric and lining fabric for cover (see cutting instructions)

Cushion pad

Buttons

Buttonhole thread

Scissors and sewing equipment

Matching sewing thread

Envelope-style cushions are best not stuffed too full, so make the cover the same size as the cushion pad and possibly remove some filling. Lining the cushion cover produces a better finish – consider featuring a narrow shirt stripe or a small geometric print that you might just be able to see as the corners of the flap turn up. See the previous page for some effective ideas on teaming decorative buttons with fabric.

MEASURING UP AND CUTTING OUT

Cut one panel 3cm (1¼in) wider than the cushion pad and twice the length plus 16cm (6¼in). Cut the lining fabric to the same dimensions.

LINING THE FABRIC

Place the lining and fabric together with right sides facing. Stitch along one short side. Stitch around the opposite end from 15cm (6in) along each side,

Right *Choose the buttons for your cushions to suit the situation. Self fabric-covered buttons are sophisticated and understated, but you might prefer contrasting colours to use the buttons as accent points.*

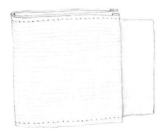

as illustrated, taking a 1.5cm (⅝in) seam allowance. Snip into the seam allowance at right angles to the raw edge, as far as the stitching, at the end of each stitching line. Snip across the corners and turn the fabric the right side out. Press.

JOINING THE SIDE SEAMS

Fold the fabric with the right sides inside, lining up the first short side with the 13.5cm (5⅜in) stitching notches. Pin

Right *A single large button is enough to fasten a loosely filled envelope-style cushion.*

the raw edges together, with enough pins to prevent any slippage – especially if using silks or velvets. Stitch these two long side seams.

FINISHING THE COVER

Snip across the corners and neaten the seams. Turn the cover the right side out, push out the corners neatly using the tip of a pair of scissors then press. Topstitch around the flap and across the other short end, about 2cm (¾in) from the edge. Make buttonholes in the flap (see

page 67) and fold it over so that you can mark the positions of the buttons. Stitch the buttons in place through the layers of fabric to secure. Insert the cushion pad and fasten the buttons to finish.

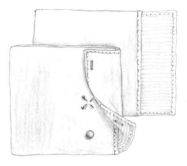

Cushions and ties

FABRIC TIES ARE a very smart way of introducing bows or knots to cushions. They can be used as cover fastenings or they can be purely decorative features. Short, wide ties can make good chunky knots at the corners of cushions and at cushion cover openings, while longer, narrower lengths of fabric may be tied in floppy bows. As for any scatter cushion, use a tied cushion on its own, as the centrepiece on a sofa or as a focal point on a bed.

Tied corner cushion

MEASUREMENTS

Size of cushion pad and finished cushion cover:
50cm (20in) square

SUGGESTED FABRICS

Glazed cotton, natural ticking, colour-woven stripes and checks

MATERIALS

Fabric for cover – 0.7m (¾yd) of 120cm (48in) wide fabric

Contrast fabric for borders/ties – 0.5m (½yd)

50cm (20in) zip to match main cushion fabric

50cm (20in) square cushion pad

Scissors and sewing equipment

Matching sewing thread

This cover has topstitched borders that tie at the corners. The cover is best made up in a medium-weight cotton fabric, selected to suit your scheme – understated when made with simple striped fabrics such as fine ticking, or elaborate with full-blown roses and complementary checks.

MEASURING UP AND CUTTING OUT

Placing any pattern to its best advantage, cut out a panel of main fabric for the front and back, each 53 × 55cm (21¼ × 22in). Cut four strips 12.5cm (5in) wide and 100cm (40in) long from contrasting fabric.

MAKING UP THE BORDERS/TIES

Fold a strip in half lengthways, right side inside. Taking a 12mm (½in) seam, stitch along the long

raw edges for 26.5cm (10⅝in) from each end. Press the seams open, moving the 'tube' of fabric so as to centre the seams along the length of the band. Stitch across each end securely. Clip the corners and turn the strip the right side out. Push out the corners using the tip of a small pair of scissors and press. Repeat with the other three strips.

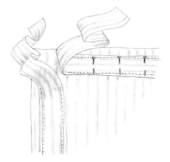

POSITIONING THE STRIPS

Align the centre of each strip with the mid-point of the panels, leaving the tails at each end. Place a length along each edge of the right side of the front panel, 2cm (¾in) in from the outside edge on three sides, 2.8cm (1⅛in) from the edge that will have the zip, and pin in place with pins set at right angles to the raw edges. Topstitch each

border/tie strip in place with stitching 3mm (⅛in) in from the strip's sides and stitching the two ties that run across the cushion, parallel with the zip, over the two side ones.

INSERTING THE ZIP

Press 2.5cm (1in) towards the wrong side along the zip opening edge of the front and the back pieces. Stitch the pieces together for 4cm (1½in) at both ends. Insert the zip (see page 66), then open up the cover halfway.

JOINING THE FRONT AND BACK

Pin the other three side seams together, right sides facing, folding the ends of the ties inside the cover so as not to catch them in the seam. Stitch around the cover exactly 1.5cm (⅝in) from the edges to avoid catching the border strips. Clip the corners and neaten the seams. Turn the cover the right side out and push out the corners using the tip of a pair of scissors. Press. Insert the cushion pad then tie each corner in double knots or tight bows.

Above *Striped ticking is used for both the cushion cover and the topstitched border ties. Cutting the panels with the fabric grain running in different directions, creates a contrast without having to introduce another fabric.*

Above *Fabric ties can be purely decorative or they can serve to keep a cushion cover closed.*

Rouleau cushion corners

For a more delicate finish than the Tied Corner Cushion (see page 36), you could make lengths of rouleau (see page 67) and insert the unstitched middle section between the front and back pieces to look like piping. If using striped fabrics, cut the border stripes in the opposite way to the cushion front so that at each side the border stripes sit at right angles to the cushion. Similarly, you could cut checks on the cross for the border strips to contrast with the front. Longer, narrower strips can be tied into double bows or loops.

Bunched cushion corners

Bunching cushion corners is a simple way to make fun floor cushions. Almost any fabric can be used for such cushions – from fine cotton to heavy chenille.

Each corner needs to be finished with tassels, knotted cords or rouleau loops – just choose the detail to suit the situation and fabric. Chenille cords and key tassels are perfect for heavy damasks and chunky weaves, for example, whereas rouleau loops and finely cut fringe tassels best complement fine linen fabrics or upholstery-weight silks.

Use large cushion pads that are at least 60cm (24in) square and preferably 75cm (30in) square. A pile of two or three of these cushions will make a comfortable seat. Make up unpiped cushion covers to the same size as the cushion pads and insert the pads.

Take each corner in turn and pinch up the excess fabric to make rounded corners and a fat cushion. Tie the fabric in place with some narrow tape or spare strips of fabric. Repeat with the other three corners until you have a plump cushion with four 'ears'. Tie these corners very tightly and knot the tape or fabric. An elastic band can be used if you find it hard to tie the corners tightly enough. Knot decorative cord and tassels around each, either crunching the ears into squashy rosettes or leaving them to stand out.

Above *An orange silk cushion, its corners tied with short lengths of ribbon for a fun, informal style of cushion, is particularly suited to floor cushions.*

Bolsters

THE BOLSTER used as a cushion to support the head at the top of the bed was the forerunner of today's softer and more comfortable pillow. Bolsters were also more formally used as decorative side cushions on early wood-framed sofas, and they are the forerunners of today's scatter cushion. In the bedroom, a firm bolster running across the width of the bed, with soft down cushions on top, is comfortable for sleeping and gives good support for reading in bed. But generally bolsters are made to look decorative. They can be feminine, frilled affairs for the bedroom but can also be made in a more formal style with piped, fringed and tasselled finishes for wooden-framed sofas or benches. Feather/down mix is the best filling for the bolster pad, since it needs to be firm enough to hold its shape.

Below *Smart piping emphasizes the shape of a firmly filled, tailored bolster at the end of a sofa.*

Tailored bolster cover

The dimensions given here are for a standard sofa bolster; adjust the measurements if you are making the bolster to fit a specific piece of furniture.

MEASUREMENTS

Size of bolster and finished cover: 46cm (18in) long × 18cm (7in) diameter. The circumference will be 55cm (22in)

SUGGESTED FABRICS

Upholstery weight fabrics: heavy cotton, linen union, velvet or brocade are all ideal

MATERIALS

Fabric for cover – 0.7m (¾yd) of 90cm (36in) wide fabric

Bolster pad – 46cm (18in) long × 18cm (7in) diameter

40cm (16in) zip

0.7m (¾yd) hand-made piping (see page 69) or ready-made flanged insertion cord

Scissors and sewing equipment

Matching sewing thread

CUTTING OUT

Cut a piece of fabric 59 × 49cm (23½ × 19¼in) (i.e. the circumference of the bolster plus 4cm (1½in) by the length of the bolster plus 3cm (1¼in). Cut two circles 21cm (8¼in) in diameter for the bolster ends, which includes a 1.5cm (⅝in) seam allowance.

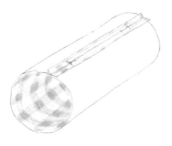

SETTING IN THE ZIP

Join the short sides of the bolster tube, taking 2cm (¾in) seams and setting a zip into the seam (see page 66). Press the seam and open the zip. Turn the tube the right side out.

ADDING THE PIPING

Pin piping or flanged insertion cord all around each end of the tube, matching the raw edge of the piping with that of the fabric. Where the piping meets, unravel the ends, twist together and neaten the fabric covering (see page 70). Stitch the piping in place.

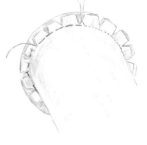

JOINING THE ENDS

Make 1.5cm (⅝in) snips at roughly 2.5cm (1in) intervals in the seam allowances around both tube ends, including the seam allowance of the piping. With right sides together, pin a circle to the snipped fabric each end of the tube, making more snips as necessary to keep the fabric flat. Baste in place. Stitch as close to the piping cord as possible. Check from the front that the stitching is as tight to the cord as possible and stitch around again, if necessary.

FINISHING THE PAD

Neaten the seams, turn the bolster the right side out and press. Insert the bolster pad, plumping it for a good fit.

Knotted bolster cover

MEASUREMENTS

Size of bolster and finished cover: 46cm (18in) long × 18cm (7in) diameter. The circumference will be 55cm (22in)

SUGGESTED FABRICS

Cotton sheeting, broderie anglaise

MATERIALS

Fabric for cover – 1.4m (1½yd) of 90cm (36in) wide fabric (any pattern in the fabric will run along the length of the bolster)

Bolster pad – 46cm (18in) long × 18cm (7in) diameter

1.2m (1¼yd) ribbon, braid or lace to edge bolster ends (optional)

Scissors and sewing equipment

Matching sewing thread

This delightful cover adds a casual, stylish touch to a bedhead bolster. It employs a French seam, which is often used for making pillowcases.

CUTTING OUT

Cut out one piece of fabric, 120 × 59cm (48 × 23 ½in), i.e. 75cm (30in) longer than the bolster by the circumference of the bolster plus 4cm (1½in).

JOINING THE SIDES

Fold the fabric in half lengthways, wrong sides together, and stitch the length of the bolster cover 6mm (¼in) from the raw edges. Trim the seam allowance, press, and continue to make a French seam (see page 65).

Right *Crisp white cotton is easy to launder and always looks fresh. Add any topstitched lace decoration being used before making up the bolster cover.*

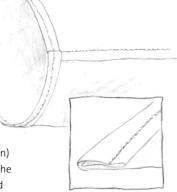

FINISHING THE ENDS

Press under 1.5cm (⅝in) double hems around each end. Stitch with a plain or a decorative stitch. Attach ribbon, braid or lace all around, if liked. Press.

FINISHING THE COVER

Insert the bolster pad and tie each end of the bolster fabric in a chunky, loose knot. Or you could make up long, fine ties in plain cotton then tie and knot them around the bolster ends to hold it in place.

Draw-string bolster cover

For a simple bolster cover, cut a piece of fabric 40cm (16in) longer than the bolster by the circumference of the bolster plus 3cm (1¼in). Fold it in half lengthways, right sides facing, and stitch along the length, taking a 1.5cm (⅝in) seam allowance. Neaten the seam, turn the bolster cover out and press. Press under a 1.5cm (⅝in) double hem at each end to form a casing. Stitch close to the fold line, leaving a 2cm (¾in) gap in each seam. Thread narrow ribbon or cord through each casing.

Insert the bolster pad in the cover, draw up the ends of the ribbon or cord and knot tightly. Tuck the knots inside the bolster cover and cover each small hole with fabric-covered buttons (see page 68), rosettes (see page 27) or heavy tassels.

Boxed cushions

BOXED CUSHIONS are useful soft furnishings. They are suitable as chair and sofa seats and backs, as loose cushions in occasional chair seats, or they can be floor cushions, window seats and head rests. Any seat cushion that is to provide long-term comfort needs depth, so the cover will need to be gussetted, turning the cushion into a 'box'.

Most fabrics are suitable, but washable fabrics are best for outdoor or heavily used chairs. Metal-framed chairs are structurally strong and look good with a brightly coloured or patterned cushion. Wicker chairs can look stunning in strong fabrics but since they have a lighter feel, they can also suit a softer stripe,

floral chintz or country check. Sofa cushions usually have piping, often of a different fabric, to emphasize the shape. Avoid too strong a contrast – choose a very hard-wearing fabric one or two tones deeper than the main fabric.

Buttoning any boxed cushion (see page 46) stops the cover moving, adds interest and a natural formality. Choose from fabric-covered buttons (see page 68) to match or contrast, carved shell or bone, or wool or cotton tufts.

Right *A boxed cushion improves the comfort of a wooden bench/sofa while another transforms a low table into a comfortable stool.*

Boxed bench cushion

MEASUREMENTS

Use a cushion pad that fits snugly in the chair, or one the size of the seat it has to go on. It may have one or more curved edges

SUGGESTED FABRICS

Most hard-wearing fabrics are suitable

MATERIALS

Fabric for cover (see cutting instructions)

Foam cushion pad (see above)

Fabric and cord for piping (see page 69) to go twice around the cushion

Zip slightly longer than cushion pad width

Scissors and sewing equipment

Matching sewing thread

MEASURING UP AND CUTTING OUT

For the cushion top and bottom, cut pieces of fabric 3cm (1¼in) larger all around than the final cushion size; cut a gusset to fit three sides and 3cm (1¼in) wider than the finished cushion depth, and one piece for the zip gusset 30cm (12in) longer than the opening end and 8cm (3¼in) wider than the depth. Cut out the pieces, allowing for matching any pattern.

POSITIONING THE PIPING

Pin the piping around top and bottom panels as for the Piped Cushion (see page 28), aligning the raw edges. Clip into the piping fabric at the corners to keep them square and overlap the fabric neatly at the join (see page 70).

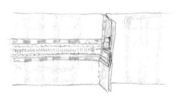

INSERTING THE ZIP

To set the zip into the gusset, cut the zip strip in half lengthways and press 2.5cm (1in) to the wrong side along both centre edges. Open up the zip and pin one side very close to the teeth. Stitch. Close the zip and place the other fold over the teeth so that the first stitching line is not visible. Pin and stitch. Join one short end of a gusset piece to the closed zip end.

SETTING IN THE GUSSET

Placing the open end of the gusset 10cm (4in) from one back corner, pin the gusset to the top piece 1.5cm (⅝in) from the raw edges, sandwiching the piping in between. At each corner, stop 1.5cm (⅝in) from the end and snip 1.5cm (⅝in) into the seam

allowance of the gusset. Fold the fabric to make a right angle and continue pinning until you reach where you started.

FINISHING THE CORNER

Unpin approximately 10cm (4in) and stitch the two gusset ends together. Repin the gusset to the top piece and stitch all around.

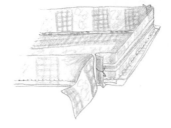

JOINING THE BOTTOM PIECE

Open up the zip about 10cm (4in) and pin the gusset to the bottom piece in the same way. Take care to match all notches and check that the corners are straight. Stitch. Turn the cover the right side out. Push out the corners neatly with the tip of a pair of scissors and press. Insert the cushion pad.

Buttoning a cushion

To button a cushion, plan the button positions straight on to the cover once the pad has been inserted. Use crossed pins to mark the button positions and a small ruler to keep each row parallel to the sides and to the next row. Ideally, the distance between buttons should form a perfect 'square' or diamond.

Mark both top and bottom of the cushion pad. If necessary, make a plan of the top side on graph paper and transfer this to the under side. You must have these marks on both sides to enable you to guide the needle through vertically.

Thread an upholsterer's needle with strong button thread. Bring the thread from underneath the cushion to the top, leaving a loose tail of thread. Thread the button on to the thread and knot. Push the needle back down through the cushion and thread on another button. Tie the two lengths of cords together and pull tightly, so that both buttons are well indented. Secure by knotting at least twice and tuck in the loose ends. Continue this process for the remaining buttons.

Tufted cushion

An alternative to studding a thin cushion with buttons is to use tufts of embroidery thread. Thread a needle with six strands of embroidery thread and stitch through the cushion from top to bottom and through to the top again. Repeat to make a second stitch in the same place. Knot the ends together and trim carefully, leaving tails of about 5cm (2in) on each end. Repeat for a fuller effect.

Left *Foam blocks covered in soft polyester wadding are substantial enough to make comfortable seats for window seats or benches.*

Above right and right

Window seats are perfect places for boxed cushions. Other types of cushion such as scatter cushions or large, firm bolsters may be added for decoration or for comfort.

Bed pillows

PILLOW COVERS are divided into two types: the pillowcase, a functional cover for the pillow used for head support while sleeping and pillow 'shams', the covers for any extra pillows used for decoration or back support.

'Housewife style' describes the cover with a flap at the back that holds the pillow in place once inserted. The edges can be plain, flat bordered, scalloped or frilled and the pillowcases are made in the same way as envelope-style scatter cushions. Pillow shams are usually open at one end with the decorated edge, whether frilled or embroidered, hanging well beyond the pillow. Large pillow covers often have only three bordered sides, with the fourth side containing the closure. A decorative pillow opening can be made with ties, buttons and rouleau loops or laces following the ideas given for scatter cushions (see pages 16–23).

Above *Like cushions, pillows can also be used decoratively rather than just for comfort. Here piled up pillows provide a good foil for bright pink cushions, which coordinate with the decorating scheme of the bedroom.*

Housewife pillowcase

MEASUREMENTS

Size of pillow (standard pillow) and finished pillowcase:
48 × 74cm (19 × 29in)

SUGGESTED FABRICS

Fine cotton, polyester cotton mix or linen. Fabric must be fully washable

MATERIALS

Fabric for pillowcase – 1.2m (1¼yd) of 115cm (45in) wide fabric

Scissors and sewing equipment

Matching sewing thread

This simple style of pillow is very straightforward to make and looks good on any style of bed.

MEASURING UP AND CUTTING OUT

Cut out one back piece of fabric 3cm (1¼in) larger all around than the pillow and one front piece 3cm (1¼in) wider and 23cm (9in) longer than the pillow, placing any pattern to its best advantage.

HEMMING THE PANELS

Stitch 1.5cm (⅝in) double hems on the right-hand side of the front and left-hand side of the back.

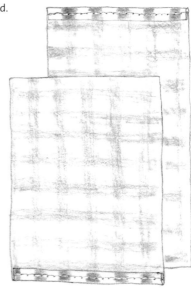

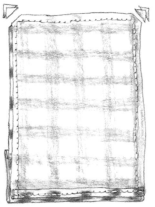

JOINING THE FRONT AND BACK
Pin the back and front pieces together, right sides facing, matching the three raw edges and folding the flap back. Stitch along the three sides. Clip the corners, neaten the seams and turn the pillowcase the right side out. Push out the corners using the tip of a pair of scissors, then press. Insert the pillow.

Above *Still the most popular pillow type, the simple housewife pillow can be made to coordinate with curtains and cushions.*

Flat border pillowcase

MEASUREMENTS

Size of pillow (standard pillow):
48 × 74cm (19 × 29in)

Size of finished pillowcase:
65 × 90cm (25½ × 35½in)

SUGGESTED FABRICS

Fine cotton, polyester cotton
mix or linen. Fabric must be
fully washable

MATERIALS

Fabric for pillowcase – 1.2m
(1¼yd) of 115cm (45in) wide
fabric

Scissors and sewing equipment

Matching sewing thread

A crisp border turns an ordinary
housewife pillow into an Oxford
pillow. The cover can be made in
the same way as the housewife
pillow, just adding extra fabric
to form the border.

MEASURING UP AND
CUTTING OUT

Cut out one back piece of fabric,
19cm (7¼in) wider than the
pillow and 13cm (5⅛in) longer.
Cut one front piece 19cm (7¼in)
wider than the pillow and
51.5cm (20½in) longer.

HEMMING THE PANELS

Stitch 1.5cm (⅝in) double hems
on the right-hand side of the

front piece and the left-hand
side of the back piece.

JOINING THE FRONT AND BACK

Pin the back and front pieces
together, right sides facing and
raw edges matching around

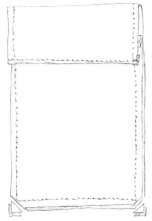

Left *Piles of pillows bring a restful atmosphere, while a mixture of shapes adds interest. Here, rectangular pillows with flat borders are teamed with a plain square scatter cushion.*

three sides. Fold a 31cm (12⅛in) wide flap at the end of the front piece back, leaving an 8cm (3¼in) border at the end. Stitch around the three sides, including the border of the front panel. Clip the corners, neaten the seams, press and turn the pillowcase the right side out. Push out the corners neatly using the tip of a pair of scissors. Press again.

STITCHING THE BORDER

Baste all around the cover, 8cm (3¼in) from the edge, taking care not to catch in the hemmed edge of the back panel. Machine stitch a decorative, plain or satin stitch along the baste lines. Remove the basting stitches and insert the pillow.

Above *Pillows have a use outside the bedroom. These soft white ones are used to soften the lines of a wooden settle and have been trimmed with red to match the flat-bordered square cushion.*

Bordered cushions

CUSHIONS WITH ADDITIONAL borders or decorative embellishments work easily together and blend well on a garden bench, piled into a squashy sofa or displayed on a bed.

While frilled edges, cords and pipings, fringes and tassels are pretty decoration and encourage a romantic and period atmosphere, padded and double borders are more modern in style and can be used on their own or with other decorative edgings. These cushion covers can be made with an Oxford-style opening (a tuck-in flap), or you can set a zip across the back of the cushion, close to the stitched edge of the border.

Double border cushion

SUGGESTED FABRICS

Cotton or linen

MATERIALS

Cushion pad

Fabric for cover (see cutting instructions)

Zip to match cushion pad width

Contrasting thread or braid to trim (optional)

Scissors and sewing equipment

Matching sewing thread

Right *A cushion cover with a double border, also known as an Oxford cushion, is extravagant with fabric, but the elegant result is well worth it.*

This style of cushion looks very effective when finished with a decorative trimming.

MEASURING UP AND CUTTING OUT

Measure the cushion pad you are using from seam to seam and cut the front piece 17cm (6¾in) wider and longer than the finished cover, and the back piece 17cm (6¾in) wider and 21cm (8in) longer. Place any pattern to its best advantage. Cut a 21.5cm (8¼in) strip from the bottom of the back piece.

INSERTING THE ZIP

Pin the two pieces for the back of the cushion together again. Stitch 2cm (¾in) from the raw edges for 19cm (7½in) from either side. Insert the zip (see page 66) and open it up halfway.

FOLDING THE BORDERS

Place the front and back pieces on the work surface in front of you, right side down. Working on each in turn, press 8.5cm (3⅜in) of each side to the wrong side.

FORMING THE MITRED CORNERS

Starting with the front piece, fold each corner under clockwise direction, as illustrated (left), in order to make a false mitre. Repeat with the back piece, also folding each corner in a clockwise direction.

JOINING THE FRONT AND BACK

Place the back and front pieces together, with wrong sides facing, so that at each corner the adjacent folds go in opposite directions. Pin then baste the panels together 7cm (2¾in) from the outside edge. Stitch decoratively all around or trim with braid and topstitch in place. Press, then insert cushion pad.

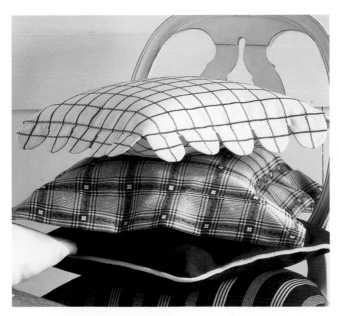

Left *Borders provide cushions with extra interest. Here, a scalloped-edged and a flat bordered cushion demonstrate two of the variations possible.*

Padded border cushion

SUGGESTED FABRICS

Glazed cotton or sateen, to show off the texture

MATERIALS

Cushion pad

Fabric for cover (see cutting instructions)

Zip to match cushion pad width

Medium-weight wadding or iron-on fleece (see padding instructions)

Contrasting sewing thread for border (optional)

Scissors and sewing equipment

Matching sewing thread

A layer of wadding or iron-on fleece adds softness to the front of the cushion and emphasizes the bordered edge.

MEASURING UP AND CUTTING OUT

Measure the cushion pad from seam to seam. To make a 5cm (2in) wide border, cut out one fabric front piece 6.5cm (2⅝in) larger all round than the cushion. Cut two back pieces: one should be a total of 14cm (5½in) wider than the cushion and 4.5cm (1⅝in) longer; the other should be the same width as the first, and a total of 14.5cm (5⅝in) in the other direction.

SETTING IN THE ZIP

Join the two back pieces with a line of basting stitches, taking 2.5cm (1in) seams, to make up a single back panel the same size as the front panel. Stitch the seam at each end for 6.5cm (2⅝in), press the seam open. Position the zip along the seam line on the wrong side of the fabric and stitch in place (see page 66). Remove the basting and open the zip slightly.

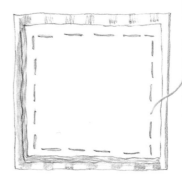

PADDING THE FRONT PANEL

Cut a piece of iron-on fleece or wadding, adding 5cm (2in) to the measurements of the cushion pad all round the edge. Centre the padding on the wrong side of the front panel. Baste the wadding in place around the edge, or fuse it to the fabric with an iron (see page 23).

JOINING THE FRONT AND BACK

With right sides facing and raw edges matching, stitch the front and back panels together all around the edge, taking care not to catch the wadding in the seam. Press, clip the corners,

turn the cushion cover the right side out. Push out the corners neatly using the tip of a pair of scissors and press again.

FINISHING THE BORDERS

Baste all around the edge of the cushion, 5cm (2in) from the seamed edge. Topstitch with a double row of stitching or a narrow satin stitch. Insert the cushion pad to finish.

Above *A single bed is transformed into an inviting sofa, with soft squashy cushions piled along the back and sides, supported by chunky bolsters at the ends.*

Children's cushions

ALL CHILDREN LOVE sitting on the floor and will enjoy bouncing around on these dice blocks or just lounging on the squashy bean bags. As the seating will get very dirty, choose easily washable fabrics in bright, strong colours to liven up a playroom. With the dice blocks, each square must be the same size. Make the first square from cardboard and use this as a template for all six sides. It is unlikely that you would make just one dice, so buy three or four different fabrics to mix and match. Order foam blocks beforehand, already wrapped in polyester wadding if possible, which gives a much softer finish.

Dice blocks

MEASUREMENTS

Size of finished dice: about 54cm (20in) square

SUGGESTED FABRICS

Heavy cottons, preferably washable

MATERIALS

Fabric for cover – 0.6m (⅝yd) of 120cm (48in) wide fabric, in each of three colours

150cm (60in) lightweight zip (optional)

50cm (20in) cube of foam

Scissors and sewing equipment

Matching sewing thread

CUTTING OUT

Cut out six squares of fabric, each 3cm (1¼in) larger all round than the dice. Plan which pieces will go around the sides and which will go top and bottom.

JOINING THE SIDES

Stitch the four sides together, taking a 1.5cm (⅝in) seam allowance and stopping the seams exactly 1.5cm (⅝in) from each end. Secure the end stitches. The tops and bottoms of each adjacent piece must line up exactly, so restitch that have slipped. Press the seams open.

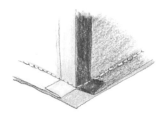

ADDING THE TOP SQUARE

To pin one side piece to the top square, position each corner so that the top of the stitching line is exactly 1.5cm (⅝in) from each side. Pin to hold, then pin between the corners, keeping the fabrics flat. Stitch, securing the stitching at each end. Repeat with the other three sides, positioning the corners first.

FINISHING THE BOTTOM

Stitch one side of the bottom square to one side piece. On the remaining six raw edges, press 1.5cm (⅝in) to the wrong side. Turn the dice cushion cover the right side out. Push out the corners neatly using the tip of a pair of scissors and press. At this point insert the zip around the three open edges if you will be using a closure. If not, insert the foam block and slipstitch the folded edges together, using buttonhole or doubled thread.

Above *Dice cushions can be made from printed fabric, or you can appliqué dots to plain fabric to make them look like real dice.*

Bean bag

MEASUREMENTS

Size of finished bean bag:
70cm (28in) across × 60cm
(24in) high

SUGGESTED FABRICS

Heavy cottons, preferably
washable

MATERIALS

2.3m (2½yd) of 150cm (60in)
wide lining fabric

1 bag of polystyrene beads
weighing 4½kg (10lb)

Total fabric for cover – 2.3m
(2½yd) of 150cm (60in) wide
fabric (see cutting instructions
if using two different fabrics)

2m (2yd) ribbon, cord or tape
for draw-string

Scissors and sewing equipment

Matching sewing thread

Right *Bean bags will provide
comfortable and versatile seating
and so are ideal for children,
students and even pets. They
are easy and inexpensive to
make, and light enough to
move around.*

This is very simple to make and
is easily removed for washing.

MEASURING UP AND CUTTING OUT

From the lining fabric, cut two
circles 73cm (29¼in) in diameter
and cut the remaining fabric to
make one strip 64 × 215cm (25¼
× 87in). Cut and join the main
fabric if necessary to make one
strip 140cm × 215cm (58 × 87in).

MAKING THE INNER BAG

For the inner bag, stitch the
short ends of the lining together,
with right sides facing, to make
a tube, leaving an 20cm (8in)
gap in the middle. Pin each
edge around one of the lining
fabric circles, snipping the fabric
as necessary to keep it lying flat.
Stitch around twice and neaten
the seams. Press. (If the side and
circles do not quite match, just
make a tuck in the side piece,
since, being the inner bag, it is
not critical.) Fill the bag with
the polystyrene beads and
machine stitch the side gap
closed. The bag should be quite
loosely filled, so that it flops
around on the floor and is
comfortable to sit in.

MAKING THE OUTER COVER

Join the short ends of the strip of main fabric to make a tube. Neaten the seam. Pin 2cm (¾in) double hems at either end. Stitch around twice, the first time close to the outside edge, and the second time close to the hemline, this time leaving a 5cm (2in) gap in each seam. Turn the right side out and press. Thread ribbon, cord or tape through one casing, pull up the loose ends and tie in a knot. Insert the bag of beads and pull up the other end of the cover in the same way.

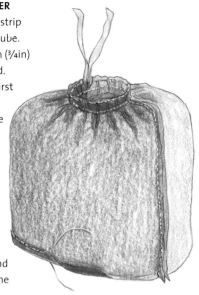

OPTIONAL TRIMMING

If you like, you can make large fabric-covered buttons (see page 68) to conceal the gathering channels at each end, or cut a circle of fabric, turn under the raw edges and slipstitch in place, as shown.

Segmented bean bag

Make up an inner lining and fill with beads as before.

Cut six sections of fabric, each 140cm (55in) long and 40cm (16in) wide. Fold one piece in half lengthways and then in half widthways. Pencil a rounded curve starting from the outside edge of the folded centre and stopping 1.5cm (⅝in) from the ends. Cut through all the layers, open out the elliptical shape you have formed and use this as a template for cutting the other five sections.

With right sides facing, stitch all the pieces together along their long sides in turn, taking care to stitch as far as the central point at the ends of each piece., and ensuring the next piece starts at the centre. There should be no holes at either end of the bean bag. Leave a 115cm (45in) gap along the last long side. Turn the cover the right side out, insert the filled lining bag, then slipstitch the opening closed.

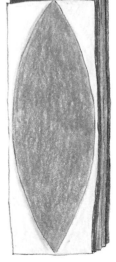

'No-sew' cushions

THE ARE WAYS of improvising and creating interesting soft furnishings, such as cushions, with either no, or very little, sewing required. Long scarves in luxury fabrics such as silk and chenille, brilliantly painted squares, woven plaids, linen tablecloths, napkins and glass cloths can all be used imaginatively to make cushion covers – and can be held in place by simple knotting, by toggles and buttons or by laces and ribbons.

Imaginative ideas

'No-sew' cushions do not need to be boring. In fact many new opportunities to incorporate imaginative designs and ideas present themselves only once the no-sewing boundary is applied. People who love sewing automatically start look at the fabric sections of department stores. They will rummage through material remnants, choose from fabric rolls and match samples with sofa and chair covers, or other cushions and curtains. The person who does not sew will need to be on the lookout for finished items, however, with an eye to clever adaptation.

Tablecloths and napkins can be buttoned together or folded and buttoned over to hold a cushion pad or a pillow – as can a towel or cot sheet. A quilt can be folded over a mattress to

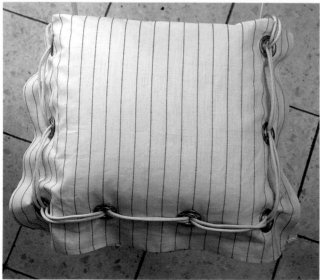

Top left *Take advantage of pre-embroidered motifs. The sides of this towel were simply stitched together to make a cushion.*

Left *Striped tea towels are laced together with sash cord through eyelet holes, the kits for which are available from most craft stores.*

make a squashy, comfortable seat cushion, and transform a bed into a useful daytime sofa. Large squares of fabric – from scarves to Indian bed covers – can be used to parcel up cushion pads, and be knotted at the front or side as part of the design.

Fastenings

Fastenings such as toggles, ribbons, laces and eyelets are all practical and can be most attractive on cushions. They may need a needle and thread to put them in place but neither a sewing machine nor any great sewing skill is necessary.

Decorative ribbons can be as narrow as 2mm (¹⁄₁₆in) or as wide as 10cm (4in) and come in all manner of styles and textures – from organdie with wired edges, tartan check and calico to double satin and unbleached linen. Buttons to suit any fabric and any situation can also be easily purchased.

Top right *A small hand towel with a teddy bear motif can be made into a child's decorative cushion with a button and ribbon fastening.*

Right *Lace panels are wrapped around a fat bolster cushion and held at either end with ribbon. A small cushion pad is covered in a tray cloth fixed in place with tiny French knots along the edges.*

Practicalities

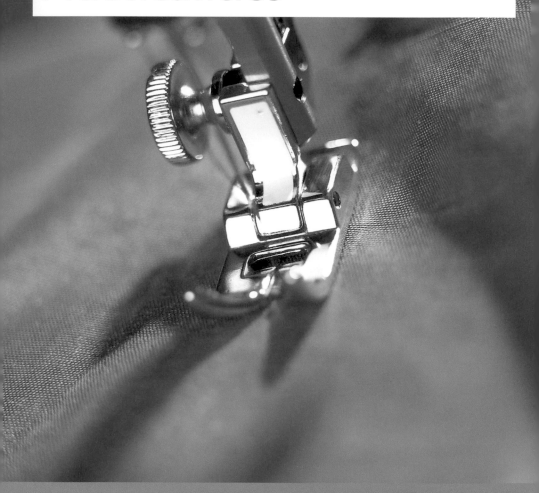

FOR SUCCESSFUL cushion-making, it is worth learning some of the sewing tips and techniques that will give your cushions that professional finish. The following pages cover sewing basics such as cutting fabric, stitching and trimming seams and adding fastenings such as zips, hooks and eyes. You can learn how to make piping and frills, both of which are widely used to define the shape of cushions and give them an attractive edge. Piping and frills can be fitted into almost any flat seam and look very effective, yet neither is difficult to make. Other decorative ideas include tips for making fabric ties, covering buttons and stitching trimmings to cushion covers.

Cutting fabric and using patterns

WHATEVER TYPE OF PROJECT you embark upon, you will need to cut out panels of fabric – usually cut on the straight grain for square cushions, or cut to shape for irregularly shaped chair cushions.

The first stage in a sewing project is marking out cutting lines and other features accurately, and then cutting the fabric. Lay the fabric out flat before starting to mark cutting lines, and ensure that it remains flat as you cut it. When cutting rectangular panels, you will get a much better finish if you are using good-quality fabric with a straight weave. If you are using patterned fabric, it should be accurately printed so that the pattern is aligned with the grain of the fabric.

Never use the selvage as the edge of a panel of fabric when sewing: the selvage may be tightly woven, preventing the fabric from falling naturally, and the unprinted selvage area may not be the width of the seam allowance required.

Pattern pieces

For some projects – a shaped chair seat for example – you may want to mark a pattern shape directly on the fabric. Alternatively, use a paper pattern as a cutting guide – brown parcel paper is good as it does not tear easily. If you are making a set of cushions, you can ensure all the pieces are the same if you draw the shape on brown paper, cut out the paper pattern, then pin the paper pattern on to the fabric so that you can cut around it. When cutting a pattern piece, make a note of whether you have included a seam allowance or not. It is sometimes easier to add the seam allowance when you cut out, by cutting 1.5cm (⅝in) away from the edge of the paper pattern.

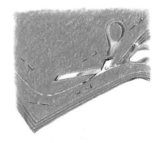

CUTTING OUT THROUGH SEVERAL THICKNESSES

If you have to cut several pieces the same shape, pin the fabric layers together and mark the pattern shape on the top piece. Cut out with the fabric laid as flat as possible. The pins will stop the layers from slipping as you cut.

Pressing and ironing

Don't regard the iron as something you use just to tidy up cushion covers (or other sewing projects) after you have made them. Pressing is an integral part of sewing. While ironing helps remove wrinkles and creases, pressing is a more precise technique: working on a small area at a time, you use the heat and steam from an iron to flatten details, lifting the iron up and down. Use the point of the iron to get into corners.

If you press your seams as you work, you will get much better results and you can attack the corners that you will not be able to get at once an item is made up.

After stitching a straight seam, press along the line of stitching, to set the stitches into the fabric, then open out the seam and press the seam allowance open from the wrong side. Pressing is particularly important for items, such as cushion covers, that need turning the right side out once stitched.

Seams

MOST SEWING will involve seams. For cushions, these may be short straight seams on square and rectangular cushions, curved seams on round cushions or bulky piped seams in tailored cushions. Some seams are decorative; others need to be invisible. For strength, most seams are stitched by machine, but in some cases you may prefer to sew by hand, using a fine running stitch or backstitch.

Before machine stitching a seam, all seam allowances must be matched carefully. Match the edges to be joined, with right sides together, and pin the layers together close to the stitching line. Position your pins at right angles to the stitching lines, so that the points just reach the seam line. If you prefer, join the layers with a row of basting stitches before stitching the seam.

Flat seams

A flat seam is commonly used for joining fabric widths. To make a seam lie flat and prevent unsightly lumps on the right side of the fabric, you may need to trim and layer the seam allowance, particularly if there are several layers of fabric. If this is the case, trim each layer a different amount, so that the edges do not all fall together when the seam is pressed. Also trim, notch and clip the seam allowances of curved seams and at corners, so that when the piece is turned the right side out, you have a smooth unpuckered curve or a crisp corner. You can also neaten the edges of a seam allowance by trimming it with pinking shears, with a zigzag or overlock stitch, by turning under and stitching the raw edges or, with a heavy fabric, you may prefer to bind the raw edges with bias binding.

STITCHING A FLAT SEAM

Stitch the seam with the fabric's right sides together and raw edges matching. Normally, a 1.5cm (⅝in) seam allowance is used. Reinforce the ends of the seam line by reverse stitching.

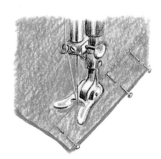

LAYERING SEAM ALLOWANCES

Trim each seam allowance in a seam by a different amount to reduce bulk. This technique is particularly important for a smooth fit on items with bulky, piped seams, such as covers for thick boxed cushions.

CLIPPING CORNERS

On a corner, such as the corner of a cushion cover, clip away the seam allowance diagonally across the corner. For very bulky and sharply angled corners, you can taper the seam allowances further, to reduce the thickness of the fabric in the corner when the cover is turned the right side out.

CLIPPING AND NOTCHING CURVED SEAMS

On an outer curve, on a circular cushion cover for example, cut little notches out of the seam allowances every 2.5–5cm (1–2in) so that when the cover is turned the right side out the fabric lies flat. On inner curves, clip into the seam allowance, so that when the item is the right side out the outer edges of the seam allowance lie flat.

French seams

In a French seam, the seam allowances are closed together to make an unsightly bulge on the reverse side. It is useful for joining fine fabrics and making pillowslips, which need frequent laundering. The seam is hard to work around corners and curves. The two layers are stitched with wrong sides together and a narrow seam; the seam allowance is then trimmed and the fabric turned so you can finish the seam from the wrong side.

STITCHING A FRENCH SEAM

Join the panels of fabric, their wrong sides together, stitching about 6mm (¼in) outside the seam line. Trim the allowance to 3mm (⅛in) from the first line of stitching. Press the first stitching line, pressing the seam allowances together. Turn the fabric to bring the right sides together, folding the fabric along the first stitching line. Stitch along the seam line, enclosing the fabric's raw edges.

Mock French seams

A mock French seam gives a similar result to a French seam, but is suitable for lightweight fabrics only. The technique makes it easier to position the main seam line accurately, and it has the big advantage that it can be used around corners. Essentially, after stitching an ordinary flat seam, the raw edges are turned inwards and stitched together.

STITCHING A MOCK FRENCH SEAM

Stitch an ordinary seam, the right sides of fabric facing. Press along the line of stitching. Turn up and press a narrow 6mm (¼in) turning down each seam allowance. Pin the turned-in edges together and stitch a line of stitching close to the folded edges of the seam allowance, through all the layers of fabric.

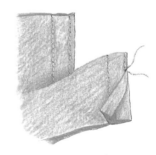

On curved seams, clip into the seam allowance before pressing and stitching the turnings.

Holding fast

MOST CUSHIONS have openings so that the cushion pad can be easily removed and the cover cleaned. Most cushion cover and some pillowcase openings need fastenings to keep them closed. Fastening by the length (touch-and-close, hook-and-eye or press-stud tape) is often used for slip covers, but zips are much more often used for cushion covers. Touch-and-close fastenings are useful on some heavy-duty items, while hooks and eyes, press studs and buttons are often more economical. Closures are often fitted in the seam lines of cushions, but it can be easier to set them across the back panel of the cover – especially where piping or frills are involved – to give a finished cushion a neatly piped outline, for example.

Fastening by the length

Nylon touch-and-close fastening comes in long strips made up of a double layer: one half has tiny hooks and the other has a soft mesh of nylon loops. When joining two fabric pieces, allow an overlap equal to the width of the fastening you are using. Also allow for turning under each of the edges to be joined. Topstitch the fastening in place to the wrong side of the overlap and the right side of the underlap. Fix lightly with glue before stitching them, as the backing is very difficult to pin in place. Use the mesh of loops on the overlap and the crisper hooks on the underlap.

Position hook-and-eye and press-stud tapes in the seam allowance or along an overlap. The eyes of the hook-and-eye tape, and the sockets of the press-stud tape, should be on the right side of the underlap; the hooks and the studs should be on the underside of the overlap. Topstitch in place. Do not stitch close to the metal or plastic inserts in the tapes.

Setting a zip in a cushion panel

Set a zip between two flat panels, close to the seam line to be less intrusive. On boxed cushions, set the zip into a side panel before making up the cushion.

JOINING THE PANELS

Decide where the zip should be in the panel. Make a paper pattern of the panel's finished dimensions and cut it along the zip line. Use the two patterns to cut out the fabric, adding 2.5cm (1in) seam allowances along the edges where the zip will be. Baste the two pieces together along the position of the zip, taking care to match patterned fabric, if appropriate. Stitch a little at each end of the seam line, leaving unstitched the part where the zip will be. Leave the seam basted along the zip line.

POSITIONING THE ZIP

Press the seam, then press the seam allowances open (along the basted section as well). Position the zip behind the seam, so that it is centred over

the basted seam line. Pin and baste in place, then, working from the right side, topstitch the zip in place, across the ends and down both sides.

Use a zip or piping foot (see page 70) to avoid damaging the zip. Do not stitch close to the zip or the fabric will gape and the zip will be difficult to operate.

Hand-sewn fastenings

Individual hooks and eyes, and press studs are sewn on by hand; and buttons are best sewn by hand for a secure finish. Mark the position of these closures carefully, and check both halves are aligned accurately before stitching in place.

HOOKS AND EYES

Stitch hooks and eyes on with several stitches around the link of each. Check the positions carefully before stitching to ensure they match up. On an overlapped closure, the hardware should not show when the fastening is closed. The eye or bar should be on the underlap.

PRESS STUDS

Align the two halves of a stud by pushing a needle through the central hole, and through both fabric layers to be joined. Stitch the stud on the overlap and the socket on the underlap.

Holes and loops

Buttonholes can be stitched by machine (see your sewing machine manual for detailed instructions for making button-holes). Rather more elaborate to make are rouleau button loops, created from a long fabric tube, which is stitched into loops down the overlapping edge of a closure. These can be spaced apart on a cushion cover or butted together for a more dramatic effect. The loops have to be set into a seam down the opening edge of the item, created by a facing of fabric.

MACHINE-STITCHED BUTTONHOLES

Buttonholes are best worked through more than one fabric layer, so allow a generous turning on the overlapping edge where you wish to stitch the buttonhole. Measure the button's diameter and mark the position and length of the buttonhole on the fabric. Use the settings on your sewing machine (some are automatic) to work the outline of the buttonhole. Use fine embroidery scissors to cut the fabric between the stitches, without cutting into them.

ROULEAU LOOPS

Each rouleau loop must be long enough to go over the button's diameter, and have seam allow-ances to stitch into the open-ing's edge. Work out each loop's length, including seam allow-ances, and cut a single strip of fabric the total length required and about 2.5cm (1in) wide.

Turn under 6mm (¼in) down each long edge, then fold in half, right sides out. Stitch down the middle to enclose the raw edges.

ATTACHING ROULEAU LOOPS

Set the rouleau loops into a faced opening, so that the raw loop ends are enclosed. Position the loops next to each other for a traditional 'buttoned dress' finish, or space them apart down the opening for less work! Pin the loops along the raw edge on the right side of the overlap, with raw edges matching. Stitch in place, then position the facing over the loops, right side down, and stitch the seam. Press, turn the facing to the inside and press again.

Fabric-covered buttons

Covered buttons look very effective with rouleau loops (see above) – small buttons for tightly spaced loops, and larger buttons for a more casual effect. They also look good used to stud a cushion (see page 46).

Cover buttons with fabric to match the cushion cover, or add plain-covered buttons to a patterned item. For extra detail, coordinate the buttons with the rouleau loops.

Button forms are available from haberdashery departments in a range of sizes, complete with instructions. If you are using very fine or slippery fabric, use iron-on interfacing (see page 23) to give the fabric a firmer finish before covering the button.

COVERING A BUTTON

Simply cut a circle of fabric a little larger than the diameter of the button (you will find precise

instructions with the button form) and tuck it over the front portion of the button before fixing the button back in place.

Fabric ties

Fabric ties (made in the same way as rouleau loops, see page 67, or as below) can be used just for decoration or for closing cushion covers. They can also be used, either stitched to cushions or in conjunction with metal eyelets, to tie cushions to metal or wooden furniture. Fabric ties need only fabric remnants to make them up. For metal eyelets, you need an eyelet hole kit, available from haberdashery departments and craft stores.

MAKING TIES

Cut each half of tie at least 25cm (10in) long, or make a double length to attach to an edge or insert in a seam – 10cm (4in) is a good width. Fold the strip in half lengthways, right sides facing, and run tape or cord along the length, close to the fold. Stitch across one end, catching the end of the tape in the seam. Stitch along the long edge of the tie with the usual seam allowance, taking care not to catch the tape.

Trim the seam allowance then pull the tape so as to turn the tie the right side out. Trim away the tape, turn under the raw ends and slipstitch the opening.

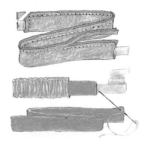

Piping and frills

STRAIGHT SEAMS and hems should usually be as invisible as possible in many soft furnishings. However, you can make a feature of seams with piping and frills, outlining an item to emphasize its shape. Even if a pattern does not give instructions for including piping or frills and flounces, they can be fitted into almost any flat seam. Bold piping or generous flounces set into seams can make a real style statement. Piping is ideal for outlining the shape of a cushion, for example, while frills of gathered fabric can be used to give a soft finish to bedroom pillows.

Making piping

Piping requires strips of fabric cut on the bias, known as bias strips or bias binding. To cover piping cord, you will need 4–5cm (1½–2in) wide strips, depending on the fabric weight and the size of the piping cord to be covered. This provides for a 1.5cm (⅝in) seam allowance, plus fabric to wrap around the cord.

Piping cord is usually made of cotton and should be preshrunk (or washed before use) if you are going to be inserting it in an item that is washable.

binding at right angles to this first line, then mark in the bias strips parallel to the first line. Cut out along the marked lines to give a number of strips.

JOINING BIAS STRIPS

Position two strips, right sides together, at right angles, their raw edges meeting. Overlap the pieces so that the corners extend on either side and you can stitch a seam line running from edge to edge and 1cm (⅜in) from the raw edges. Press the stitching, then press the seam open and trim away the corners. Wrap the bias strips around the piping cord, then stitch as close as possible to the cord, through both fabric layers.

STITCHING PIPING IN PLACE

Position the covered piping on the right side of one piece of fabric, so that the piping stitching line matches the fabric's seam line and the raw edge of the piping covering is towards the raw edge of the fabric. Stitch in place, using a piping foot on the sewing machine (see page 70), adjusted so that the needle is between the foot and the piping cord. Then position the second panel of fabric on top of the piping, right side inwards, and stitch again along the same seam.

MARKING AND CUTTING BIAS STRIPS

Take a rectangle of fabric and mark a diagonal, at a 45° angle to the selvage, from one corner across to the opposite edge. Measure the width of the

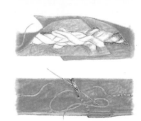

TURNING CORNERS

Where the piping goes around a corner, stitch in place as far as the corner, then snip into the seam allowance of the piping covering at the corner point, so that you can turn it around the corner. If the corner is gently curved, make several cuts into the seam allowance so that you can ease it into position.

JOINING ENDS OF PIPING

After pinning piping in place, cut the ends of fabric diagonally (following the fabric grain) and cut off the piping cord, leaving a 1.5cm (⅝in) seam allowance at each end. Unravel the piping cord at the overlap and entwine the loose ends together. Turn under the binding seam allowances and slipstitch together.

RUCHED, OR GATHERED, PIPING

This gives a sumptuous finish to seams. Use the heaviest piping cord you can find. Cut the fabric for binding the piping on the straight grain or the bias; its width should be at least eight times the diameter of the cord. Cut the cord and binding to one and a half times the finished length of the seam to be piped. Wrap the binding around the cord and baste in place. Stitch 3–6mm (⅛–¼in) from the cord. Stitch across one end of the piping, through the cord and binding to secure it. Slide the binding down the cord. When sufficiently gathered, stitch across the open end of the binding to hold the cord in place, and trim away the extra cord.

Stitching a zip or piping

Use the narrow zip/piping sewing machine foot to stitch near a zip's teeth. The foot can be adjusted to stitch on each side. The narrow foot is also used to stitch binding closely in place around piping cord or to stitch the covered cord to fabric in a seam.

Frills and flounces

Frills of matching or contrasting fabric can be inserted into seams around the edge of a cushion. For an inserted frill, a folded strip of fabric is usually used, which saves hemming; a topstitched frill needs its raw edges finished before you gather and stitch the frill. Decide how wide you want

the frill before cutting the fabric: for a cushion, 40cm (16in) square, you need a finished frill at least 5cm (2in) wide.

PREPARING THE FRILL

Cut a strip of fabric that is equal in width to twice the width of the finished frill, plus seam

allowances. The frill length should be 1½–2 times the length of the finished seam. Neaten the ends of the frill by folding the strip in half lengthways, wrong sides together. Stitch the short seams at each end, press, trim the seam allowances and turn the right side out. Push out the corners neatly using the tip of a pair of scissors then press the frill.

GATHERING THE FRILL

Gather the frill with machine or running stitch. If you are using running stitch, make two rows of stitches, quite close to each other, staggering the positions of the stitches to prevent pleats from forming.

Draw up the gathers until the gathered frill length matches the length of the seam where it is to be stitched. Anchor the gathering threads around a pin at each end of the frill. Check that the fullness is evenly distributed along the frill and pin or baste it in place on the fabric panel.

SETTING IN THE FRILL

Begin by stitching the frill to the right side of one of the fabric panels, with raw edges matching, making sure that the fullness is distributed evenly. Position the second fabric layer (normally the back of the cushion cover) right side inwards, over the frill and stitch the seam. Press, trim the seam allowances and turn the fabric to the right side. Allow extra fullness at corners where the frill extends around the corners of a cushion cover.

PIPED AND FRILLED FINISH

For extra detail, combine piping with a frill in a seam. Position the piping along the raw edge of the top panel, and stitch in place. Then position the gathered frill and stitch. Finally position the back panel of fabric, so that the

piping and frill are sandwiched in place. Stitch the seam. Trim all seam allowances, press and turn the fabric to the right side.

TOPSTITCHED FRILL

Cut the fabric for the frill to th width of the desired finished frill, plus a turning allowance. The length of the fabric strip should be 1½–2 times the gathered length of the frill. Turn under the hems all round and stitch, using a fine zigzag stitch or make a double hem. Gather the frill along the stitching line as before, then topstitch it in place on the fabric panel, distributing the fullness evenly.

Decorative extras

THERE ARE MANY different braids, fringing, cords and ribbons available for adding decorative detail to soft furnishings without having to cut and prepare custom-made piping and frills. A look round a haberdashery department will give you many ideas for ready-made finishes. Some are intended for setting into seams in the fabric, others are topstitched in place before making up an item. Silky, rope-twist insertion cord, which has a flange woven into it to stitch into the seam, gives a luxurious touch to scatter cushions; woven braids can be stitched to the top panel of a cushion, while fringing can emphasize cushion edges.

Finishes for seams and hems

Flanged insertion cord is used in the same way as covered piping cord, to emphasize seam lines. Position it along the seam line of the main panel of fabric, and stitch it in place with a piping foot (see page 70), taking care to stitch only the flange and not the cord itself. Position the second panel of fabric on top to complete the seam.

USING INSERTION CORD
Stitch the flanged cord in place to the right side of one panel of fabric, just as for stitching piping in place (see page 69), before completing the seam.

COPING WITH CORNERS
If the insertion cord has to fit around a curve or corner, first clip into the flange so you can then more easily manoeuvre the cord into place.

Topstitched finishes

When applying a topstitched finish, such as braid, fringing, ribbon or lace, it is important to measure and mark accurately. The decoration should be applied before making up an item such as a cushion cover. This makes it easier to work and, where the trimming runs to the item's edge, you can be sure that the raw edges will be stitched into the seam as you make up the cushion cover.

MARKING THE POSITION
Mark the position of the trimming on the fabric with tailor's chalk. Decide whether to align the trimming centrally, or to one side of the line.

Cut a length of the trimming to match the marked line, ensuring that you allow at least 12mm (½in) for turning under at each end.

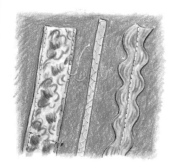

TOPSTITCHING

Pin and baste the trimming in place, then topstitch it by machine. Wide trimmings should be topstitched close to each edge with straight stitching, or use a narrow zigzag stitch worked over the trimming's edge. If you are making two lines of stitching, work them both in the same direction to avoid twisting and distorting the trimming. Very narrow trimmings can be held in place with a single line of straight or zigzag stitching along the trimming's centre.

TURNING A CORNER

On cushions, you may want to add a square or rectangle of ribbon or braid, topstitched in place, which involves mitring the corners. Mark the outer line of the rectangle as a guide for positioning the trimming. Topstitch the trimming in place along the outer edge, stopping at the corner. Reverse stitch to strengthen the stitching, then remove the fabric panel from the machine. Fold the trimming back on itself at the corner and machine stitch a short, diagonal seam across the trimming, from the outer corner down to the trimming's inner edge, as shown. Clip away the seam allowance, if necessary. Press flat, then continue stitching to the next corner. When complete, topstitch the inner edge of the trimming in place.

Embroidered touches

Embroidered details can turn an ordinary accessory into something special. If you have an electronic sewing machine with embroidery programmes, you will have no difficulty in finding suitable motifs and letters. To embroider an item by hand, select a suitable motif – perhaps a cartoon character for a child's floor cushion – and then select stitches to suit the pattern.

Decorative stitches

Hand embroidery stitches are always worked from the right side of the fabric to see the finished effect. With most fabrics, you need to stretch the area you are working on over an embroidery hoop. With an even tension on the fabric, you can keep an even stitch tension.

Cross stitch forms the basis of canvaswork embroidery, and is also used on linens and cottons. For a design with large areas of colour, use satin stitch or long and short stitch for very large areas, where the satin stitch might pull into loops with wear.

French knots can create spot details – the eyes on a face or the pollen in a flower, for example.

USING EMBROIDERY COTTON

Stranded embroidery cotton comes in six strands, loosely twisted together. Cut off a short working length – 30cm (12in) is ideal – and divide the thread into two sets of three strands, unless you are working with a very chunky fabric.

Facts and figures

CHOOSE TO WORK in either imperial or metric, but do not mix the measurements. For quick reference, a series of conversion charts is given below: detailed conversions of small amounts, fabric yardage/metrage and common fabric widths. These last two charts are for use in stores that sell by the metre when you have worked out quantities in yards.

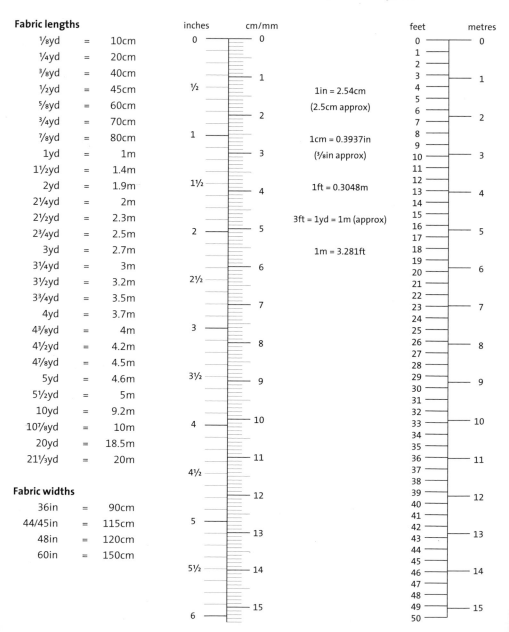

Fabric lengths

⅛yd	=	10cm
¼yd	=	20cm
⅜yd	=	40cm
½yd	=	45cm
⅝yd	=	60cm
¾yd	=	70cm
⅞yd	=	80cm
1yd	=	1m
1½yd	=	1.4m
2yd	=	1.9m
2¼yd	=	2m
2½yd	=	2.3m
2¾yd	=	2.5m
3yd	=	2.7m
3¼yd	=	3m
3½yd	=	3.2m
3¾yd	=	3.5m
4yd	=	3.7m
4⅜yd	=	4m
4½yd	=	4.2m
4⅞yd	=	4.5m
5yd	=	4.6m
5½yd	=	5m
10yd	=	9.2m
10⅞yd	=	10m
20yd	=	18.5m
21⅓yd	=	20m

Fabric widths

36in	=	90cm
44/45in	=	115cm
48in	=	120cm
60in	=	150cm

1in = 2.54cm
(2.5cm approx)

1cm = 0.3937in
(⅜in approx)

1ft = 0.3048m

3ft = 1yd = 1m (approx)

1m = 3.281ft

Glossary

Acrylic Synthetic fibre used to make fabric that has similar properties to wool.

Appliqué Method of decorating fabric by stitching on shapes cut from other fabrics.

Basket weave Woven effect in fabric with several strands of warp and weft threads running together to create a small block effect.

Binding (bias and straight cut) Narrow strips of fabric used to cover the edge of a larger panel of fabric; bias binding is cut diagonally across the fabric (on the bias) so that it can be eased around curves without pleats and puckers.

Bouclé Yarn spun with a loose, looped finish; fabric woven or knitted from bouclé yarn.

Bound button holes Tailored buttonholes finished with strips of fabric binding, rather than machine or hand-sewn buttonhole stitch.

Braid Woven trimming, used for topstitched decorations on cushion covers and other soft furnishings; braids are more substantial, and often more elaborately woven, than ribbons.

Brocade Medium- to heavyweight fabric, woven in two colours to make a satin background with a relief pattern.

Broderie anglaise Cotton fabric that has been pierced and embroidered to create a decorative effect; available as a full-width fabric and as a narrow trim; usually white or cream in colour.

Button loops Fabric or hand-stitched loops that act as button holes. Fabric button loops are also known as rouleau loops

Calico Medium-weight cotton cloth, usually white or unbleached; its low price makes it suitable for making cushion pads with foam or polyester stuffing.

Canvas Heavyweight cotton fabric, often used for deck chair covers.

Canvaswork Embroidery, usually in wool, on special even-weave, holey canvas.

Casing A channel in a piece of fabric made by folding over the top and making two lines of stitching; used to make draw-string bags, curtain headings, etc.

Check A grid pattern, usually woven but may be printed on to fabric.

Chenille Subtly ribbed, velvety fabric, softer in texture than velvet or corduroy.

Chintz From a Hindu word, chintz is a printed cotton fabric, usually glazed (glossy), but the term is now used to denote any glazed cotton fabric.

Clip To cut into fabric at right angles to the raw edge, or diagonally across corners, to prevent distortion of curved seams and bulk in corners when an item is turned the right side out.

Complementary colours Colours on opposite sides of the colour wheel: red and green; blue and orange; yellow and purple.

Corduroy Heavyweight fabric with pile woven into the fabric to form narrow ribs.

Covered buttons Buttons covered with fabric; they can be made with special button forms, available from haberdashery departments and stores.

Crewel work Flowing style of embroidery, developed in 16th-century Europe, usually in wool on linen.

Damask Fabric (usually silk or linen) with a pattern woven into it; often woven in a single colour, so that the pattern only shows as the light catches the fabric.

Denim Originally from the city of Nîmes in France, a twill weave fabric traditionally woven using indigo warp and white weft threads.

Dobby weave Fabric woven with small, repeating pattern, like a diamond or raised star.

Domette Soft fabric, often synthetic, used as a layer of padding in curtains or under table-cloths.

Dressmaker's carbon paper Paper with coloured coating on the back, so that when you trace an outline on it the motif is transferred to a layer of fabric placed beneath the carbon paper.

Duck Originally used for sails and outerwear, this plain weave fabric in cotton or linen is hard-wearing, and can be used for loose covers.

Easy-care fabrics Usually woven from a mix of fibres, and requiring minimal ironing.

Electronic sewing machine Electric sewing machine with microchips to make it easy to adjust the type, size and tension of the stitch.

Facing Panel of fabric used to back the main fabric of a cushion or other item around the opening, giving a neat finish.

Faille Silk fabric with a ribbed weave.

Felt Non-woven, non-fraying textile, tradition-ally in wool, with many craft applications.

Field The background colour of a printed or embroidered piece of fabric.

Flat seam A simple seam used to join two pieces of fabric with a single line of stitching.

French seam Double seam in which the raw edges are completely enclosed.

Geometric print Regular print, of abstract shapes arranged in a regular pattern.

Gingham Lightweight woven fabric, usually white and one other colour, originally a striped fabric, but now used to describe check.

Grain of fabric The lengthways grain is the direction in which the warp threads of the fabric run, parallel to the selvages.

Ground The 'background' fabric used in appliqué, embroidery, etc.

Gusset A narrow panel, sometimes shaped or gathered to give fullness; the side panels of a box-shaped cushion.

Herringbone A fine, hand-sewn stitch, used to join panels of wadding or to hold hems in place; may also be used as an embroidery stitch.

Housewife pillowcase Pillowcase made with an internal flap at the open-ing end so that the pillow can be tucked in place.

Ikat Fabric woven from predyed yarn; the yarn is coloured in sections so that predyed patches are woven in next to each other to create a pattern.

Interfacing Layer of fabric, often synthetic, non-woven and iron-on, used to stiffen light-weight fabrics and make them easier to handle. In soft furnishings it may be used to stiffen fabrics used for appliqué motifs.

Interlining Soft fabric (usually domette or bump) used in lined cur-tains or tablecloths for added weight and luxury.

Jacquard Fabric with colour-woven pattern, similar to brocade or damask, taking its name from the inventor of the loom on which it is woven.

Lapped seam Seam made by overlapping the edges of the panels of fabric to be joined.

Lawn Fine plain-weave cotton fabric.

Layer To trim the seam allowances within a seam to different lengths, eliminating bulk.

Linen union Plain weave fabric made from a mix-ture of linen and cotton threads.

Lining Layer of fabric added to give improved wear.

Liséré Embroidered and beribboned or elaborately woven fabrics and trimmings.

Lycra Brand name for a stretch fibre (elastane).

Matelasse Padded cushion or mattress.

Mercerized cotton thread Sewing thread specially treated to improve wear and look more lustrous.

Monochromatic scheme Colour scheme that uses only one colour (plus white) in varying tones.

Monotones Scheme using only one tone of a colour.

Motif Abstract or figurative outline or pattern on printed or woven fabric, or pattern used for embroidery, appliqué, etc.

Muslin Fine, loosely woven cotton fabric, commonly in white or natural.

Notch To cut a V-shaped wedge out of the seam allowance; this is done so that pieces of fabric can be matched when they are being stitched together, and also to reduce bulk in curved seams when an item is turned the right side out.

Organdie Fine stiff cotton, open-weave fabric, now often available in synthetic fibres.

Organza Finely woven stiff silk, made from a particular type of twisted silk yarn.

Ottoman Heavy, twill-weave fabric, in silk, linen, cotton or synthetic fibre.

Overlock machine Advanced sewing machine that forms stitches in a more elaborate way than a traditional sewing machine; particularly useful for stretch fabric.

Oxford pillowcase Housewife pillowcase with a wide, flat border extending all around the edge.

Paisley An intricate pattern with elongated and curved oval motifs, originating in India but taking its name from the Scottish town renowned for its textile industry.

Petersham ribbon Hard-wearing, ribbed ribbon, traditionally made of silk.

Petit point Fine cross stitch, worked in wool on needlepoint canvas.

Pile The 'fur' of a carpet or of a velvety fabric.

Piqué Light- or medium-weight cotton fabric woven in a single colour with a fine, embossed effect.

Plaid Colour-woven fabric (a check).

Polyester wadding Thick, soft, lightweight padding available in standard widths and thicknesses.

Primary colours The three basic colours – red, blue and yellow – from which all other colours can be mixed (with the addition of black and white).

Provençal print A small, geometric interpretation of paisley patterns, printed in strong colours on lightweight plain-weave cotton.

Pucker Unsightly gathering along a seam line, caused by a blunt needle or a bulky seam.

PVC A plastic coating applied to fabrics to make them waterproof and wipeable.

Rayon A synthetic fibre – the first one to be developed – that imitates silk.

Rouleau A fine tube of fabric, used to make button loops.

Ruching Gathering fabric to create a panel of luxurious folds.

Sateen Cotton fabric woven to produce a glossy effect.

Satin A type of weave in which warp threads run over the surface of the fabric to give a glossy finish; a silk fabric with a satin weave.

Satin stitch Closely worked stitch; may be worked in lines by sewing machine or over larger areas by hand.

Scrim Stiff, loosely woven lightweight linen fabric.

Seam allowance The allowance around the edge of a piece of fabric for making a seam. Add a seam allowance to the finished dimensions before cutting out the fabric.

Seam line The marked or imaginary line around the edge of a piece of fabric marking the line of stitching when a seam is made.

Seam tape Firmly woven narrow cotton tape used to prevent seams from distorting; the seam tape is positioned along the seam line on the wrong side of the fabric, and stitched into the seam as the layers of fabric are joined.

Secondary colours The three colours – purple, green and orange – obtained by mixing any two primary colours.

Seersucker Plain woven fabric, often striped or checked, in which groups of warp and/or weft threads are drawn tighter, creating rows of ruching down or across the fabric.

Selvage The woven, non-fraying edges of a length of fabric.

Serging machine *See* overlock machine.

Shot silk Silk fabric woven with different colours for the warp and weft, creating a fabric that reflects different shades as it catches the light.

Silk dupion Fabric made from silk spun by a particular type of silk-worm: two silkworms spin a double cocoon producing a double thread that can be unravelled for weaving.

Squab Small cushion tied to the seat of an upright chair.

Taffeta Plain fabric, usually silk, with a glossy, stiff finish.

Take-up lever Lever on sewing machine that moves up and down to allow the thread to loop through the fabric as you stitch.

Tarlatan Stiffened fabric, similar in weight to muslin.

Tartan Originating in Scotland, tartan is wool fabric woven to create a checked design; each clan or family traditionally had its own particular tartan.

Template A pattern; when cutting repeated identical shapes, for appliqué or patchwork, the template is cut out in card so that it can be used over and over again.

Tertiary colours Colours containing all of the three primary colours.

Thread count The number of threads in a specified area (a square inch) of a woven fabric.

Ticking Tightly woven fabric with a distinctive woven stripe;

traditionally feather-proof with black and off-white stripes, but now available in a range of natural and muted colours.

Toile de Jouy Cotton fabric, originating in 18th-century France, with figurative scenes printed in a single colour on a neutral background.

Topstitching A bold line of stitches used to emphasize seams or finish hems.

Touch-and-close fastening Synthetic fastening, made with plastic loops on one half, which link into a furry pile stitched to the opposite side of the opening.

Towelling Woven fabric with a looped pile on both sides.

Trim To cut away excess fabric.

Tussah Silk spun from the cocoons of a particular type of silkworm that feeds on oak leaves.

Twill (weave) A weave in which the warp threads

form a diagonal rib over the surface of the cloth.

Velvet Woven fabric with a pile; may be made from a wide range of fibres.

Warp The threads that run up and down a woven piece of cloth.

Weft The threads running across a woven piece of cloth.

Welt A name given to the gusset or side panel of a boxed cushion.

Wild silk Silk fabric made from natural silk fibre, but not from the *Bombyx mori* (mulberry silkworm) native to China.

Yarn Thread (natural or man-made fibre) that has been spun or twisted so that it can be woven or used for embroidery or knitting.

Index

Acknowledgements

Photography

Laura Ashley Home Autumn/Winter 2000
Collection back cover bottom left, 4 bottom, 26
The Conran Shop Ltd 1 top, 25 bottom
Crown Paints 50
Anna French Ltd 52, 57, 59
Octopus Publishing Group Ltd. 45
    Nadia Bryant 31
    Rupert Horrox front cover top, 18, 21, 28, 38, 49
    Di Lewis 8, 16 right 27 left
    David Loftus 3, 7 centre, 7 bottom, 10, 12
    bottom, 33 bottom
    Peter Myers front cover bottom, 4 top, 5
    bottom, 6, 9 bottom, 19, 28 right, 35, 47 top, 47
    bottom, 51
    David Parmitter 2, 9 top, 17, 23, 27 right, 34, 36,
    43, 60 top, 61 top, 61 bottom
    Paul Ryan 1 bottom, 24 top, 25 top, 29 left, 40
    John Sims 7 top
    Debi Treloar 5 top, 11, 13 top, 13 bottom, 14, 24
    bottom, 32, 33 top, 39, 60 bottom, 62
    Polly Wreford 12 top, 16 left
The Interior Archive
    Tim Beddow 55
    Simon Brown 20
Osborne & Little plc 46
Sahco Hesslein 30
Sanderson 53

For Hamlyn

Editorial Manager: Jane Birch
Senior Designer: Claire Harvey
Project Manager: Jo Lethaby
Designer: Mark Stevens
Picture Researcher: Christine Junemann
Senior Production Controller: Louise Hall
Illustrator: Jane Hughes